# Active History

# Civil War

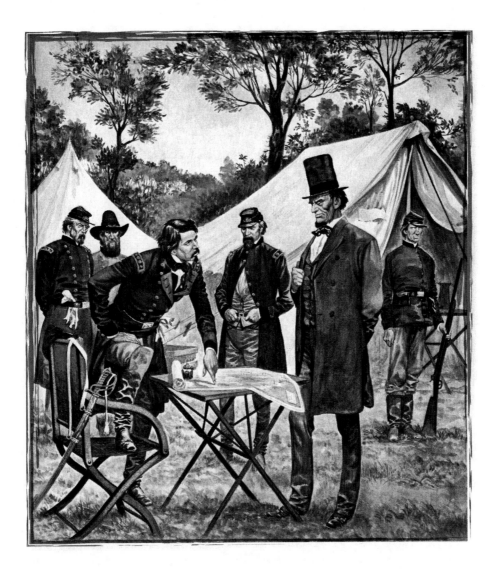

**Authors**

Andi Stix, Ed.D., and PCC
Frank Hrbek, M.A.

# SHELL EDUCATION

## Contributing Author

Wendy Conklin, M.S.

## Publishing Credits

Robin Erickson, *Production Director*; Lee Aucoin, *Creative Director*;
Timothy J. Bradley, *Illustration Manager*; Sara Johnson, M.S.Ed., *Editorial Director*;
Maribel Rendón, M.A.Ed., *Editor*; Kenya Wilkinson, M.A.T, *Editor*; Grace Alba, *Designer*;
Corinne Burton, M.A.Ed., *Publisher*

## Image Credits

Cover Bridgeman Art; p. 13 [LC-USZ62-5092], p. 60 [LC-DIG-stereo-2s02857], p. 61 [LC-USZ62-100787],
p. 62 [LC-DIG-ppmsca-35451], p. 63 [LC-LOT 9934, p. 26], p. 96 [LC-DIG-pga-02157], p. 97 [LC-USZ62-61636] Library of Congress;
pgs. 119-121 Stephanie Reid; all other images Shutterstock

## Standards

© 2004 Mid-continent Research for Education and Learning (McREL)
© 2007 Teachers of English to Speakers of Other Languages, Inc. (TESOL)
© 2007 Board of Regents of the University of Wisconsin System.  World-Class Instructional Design and Assessment (WIDA).  For more information on using the WIDA ELP Standards, please visit the WIDA website at www.wida.us.
© 2010 National Council for the Social Studies (NCSS)
© 2010 National Governors Association Center for Best Practices and Council of Chief State School Officers (CCSS)

### Shell Education

5301 Oceanus Drive
Huntington Beach, CA  92649-1030
http://www.shelleducation.com

**ISBN 978-1-4258-1174-7**
© 2014 Shell Educational Publishing, Inc.

# Table of Contents

# Research and Introduction

According to the position statement of the National Council for the Social Studies, "there is a profound difference between learning about the actions and conclusions of others, and reasoning one's way toward those conclusions. Active learning is not just 'hands-on,' it is 'minds-on'" (NCSS 2008).

The *Active History* series is designed to bring history to life in the classroom by providing meaningful experiences that allow students to learn the story behind the history. This book, *Active History: Civil War*, presents five exciting simulations. Classroom activities, in combination with the assignment and the written work needed to prepare for the simulations, will enhance each student's knowledge of a period in American history which saw infighting that pitted American against American in pursuit of defeating one another by any means necessary.

## Understanding Active Learning

Active learning provides "engagement in learning; the development of conceptual knowledge and higher-order thinking skills; a love of learning; cognitive and linguistic development; and a sense of responsibility or 'empowerment' of students in their own learning" (Lathrop, Vincent, and Zehler 1993, 6). In essence, active learning inspires students to engage meaningfully in the content and take responsibility for their learning. It involves students as active participants in the learning process while incorporating higher-order thinking.

In the classroom, active learning can take on many forms. It often encompasses collaboration, various forms of grouping students through the learning process, independent-learning opportunities, and creative methods of output to demonstrate students' learning. An important feature in active-learning classrooms is that the students are the ones in the lead while the teacher acts as the coach. Some concrete examples are provided in the chart on the following page.

# Research and Introduction *(cont.)*

| Active Learning | |
|---|---|
| **Example** | **Nonexample** |
| Students are out of their seats, collaborating with peers on a project. | Students listen to a lecture. |
| Students use various forms of communication, like podcasting, to share their ideas with others. | Students quietly write responses to questions, using complete sentences. |
| Students use manipulatives to build models to demonstrate what they learned. | Students work written problems on a worksheet to show what they have learned. |
| Students create movie trailers to summarize a book they just read. | Students write a one-page book report. |
| Students participate in small-group discussions in efforts to produce ideas for solving a problem. | Students individually read research material and take notes. |
| Students use their bodies to act out a scene and demonstrate a newly learned concept. | Students give a two-sentence ticket-out-the-door reflection on what they learned. |
| Students are presented with higher-order questions that challenge their views and must consult other documents before answering. | Students answer lower-level questions over material they read to ensure basic comprehension. |
| Students work with primary-source documents to piece together details and clues about an event in history. | Students read a textbook to understand an event in history. |

(Adapted from Conklin and Stix 2014)

Although many of the nonexamples make up pieces of typical classroom experiences and can support student learning when used appropriately and sparingly, they are not inherently active and will not produce the same depth and rigor of learning that the active learning practices do. Active learning produces more engaging opportunities for learning, and when students are more engaged, they spend more time investigating that content (Zmuda 2008).

# Research and Introduction *(cont.)*

The simulations in *Active History: Civil War* are grounded in making the students active participants in their own learning. They call for students to work in a variety of different groups to foster collaboration and communication and are designed to make students full participants who are good decision makers and competent problem solvers.

*Active History: Civil War* also challenges students to develop speaking skills and the intellectual dexterity to debate and make speeches while being asked to take part in discussions, simulations, and/or debates. They learn to think systematically, to accept other viewpoints, and to tolerate and understand others. They are also encouraged to make their own investigations and to explore all areas of study to the fullest. In this way, they learn to rely on many inquiry methods to search and probe everywhere from the local library to the Internet. Students learn to rely on relevant documents, diaries, personal journals, photographs, newspaper articles, autobiographies, and contracts and treaties as well as period songs, art, and literature in order to support their active engagement and deep learning of the content.

## Higher-Order Thinking Skills to Support Active Learning

A key component of active learning is the use of higher-order thinking skills. In order for students to be college- and career-ready, they need to be able to use these thinking skills successfully. Students use higher-order thinking when they encounter new or unfamiliar problems, questions, scenarios, or dilemmas (King, Goodson, and Rohani 1998). By structuring classroom practices that support students' use of higher-order thinking skills, you help them develop the necessary tools to be independent, creative, metacognitive, solution-driven individuals who can apply those skills outside the classroom.

Critical and creative thinking are the two key elements of higher-order thinking. Critical thinking entails one's careful analysis and judgment and "is self-guided, self-disciplined thinking which attempts to reason at the highest level of quality in a fair-minded way" (Scriven and Paul 1987). In support of this is creative thinking, which Heidi Hayes Jacobs (2010) suggests goes beyond reasonable and logical thinking. In fact, creativity is really a result of hard work and intentional thought, not luck or "magic" (Michalko 2006).

The simulations included in this book encourage students to think both critically and creatively to make decisions and solve problems. For example, students will work with primary-source materials, compose their own solutions and compare them to those that were actually made, and learn the celebrated and harsh realities of life during this period in history. Every part of *Active History* heightens the level of learning about a time in the past and helps students build their ability to apply their knowledge from language arts and other content areas to successfully complete each simulation.

# Research and Introduction *(cont.)*

## Using Simulations in the Active Classroom

A simulation is a teaching strategy that provides students with information based on an actual situation in time. It allows them to assume roles within the circumstances. By doing so, they analyze, make modifications to, and bring the event into current times. Students present differing points of view or solve the problem(s) involved in the situation. In looking at the qualities of an active-learning classroom, simulations are a great way to support students' independent learning, collaboration, communication, and active engagement in the social studies classroom.

Every simulation in this resource has students working together and going through group decision-making processes. Students are encouraged to use the Internet and other resources to support their learning. Brainstorming is a key function in many simulations. Initially, it generates concepts and ideas without judgment, speaking one's mind as well as listening to what others have to say, and, finally, narrowing the choices to fulfill the requirements of the lesson. Students voice their opinions and share their ideas as they go through the give-and-take of negotiating, compromising, and working out the final decision.

However, the learning process does not come to a stop at the conclusion of a particular simulation. Much of what students learn is useful information that can be transferred to a personal level. It is equally salient for students to see how the information affects their community and society. Therefore, the units often require students to seek out current information at the local level. Many of the lessons utilize opposing points of view. In the course of the lesson, speeches, dramatizations, debates, discussions, and written documents express these differing points of view. At the very least, the students come away with the understanding that there are at least two sides to every story. But more importantly, they also learn to be tolerant. If they speak well for their side on a particular issue, they must also listen well and have respect for the opposition. If any lesson in this unit instills in young minds tolerance, respect, civility, courtesy, understanding, and acceptance, we will have reached our goal.

## Assessment

Assessment is a key part of instruction in any of today's classrooms. The results of assessments should be used to inform instruction and support students' future learning. It is important for students to understand how they will be assessed in order to truly allow them ownership over their learning. A collection of sample rubrics can be found on the Digital Resource CD and can be easily modified to meet the needs of students. To support student success in the classroom, negotiable contracting is crucial. Student input should be included when designing assessments.

# Research and Introduction *(cont.)*

To support the implementation of negotiable contracting, follow these steps:

1.  Ask students to imagine that they are the teacher and that they will be creating a list of criteria that should be used for assessing one another's ability to speak and behave properly during the simulation.

2.  Have students work individually to create their own list.

3.  Divide students into cooperative groups and allow them to share their ideas and consolidate their lists.

4.  Call on a spokesperson from a group to submit one idea and record that idea on a sheet of chart paper.

5.  Repeat this process, rotating from group to group. Once an idea is listed, it may not be restated again by another group. Allow students to use a checkmark on their lists for ideas shared by other groups. This skill is called *active listening*.

6.  if the students have not thought of a certain criterion that you think is important and meaningful, add the item to the list and explain your reasoning to the class.

7.  List the results on large chart paper as a reference guide and post it in a visible area of the classroom.

8.  Negotiate with your students to agree on four or five of the criteria to use for assessment.

Sample suggestions for a class debate or discussion may be:

- Actively speaks and participates in discussion that demonstrates the understanding of the case
- Responds to another speaker who demonstrates comprehension of subject matter
- Asks quality questions that demonstrate logical thought
- Refers to his or her notes or any text with pertinent information
- Discusses the topic critically and tries to evaluate the topic from the particular time period

# Research and Introduction *(cont.)*

## Teacher as Coach

In the past, teachers have been defined as facilitators. But today, the new defined role of a teacher is one of a coach who offers inspiration, guidance, and training, and one who enhances students' abilities through motivation and support (Stix and Hrbek 2006).

The goal of a teacher coach is to increase student success by helping students:

- Find their inner strengths and passions in order to nurture self-worth and identity,
- Have a voice in their own learning and negotiate collectively with the instructor to create the goals and objectives,
- Passionately engage in discussion about content to increase memory retention and fuel motivation to learn,
- Use their inner talents to bring their work to the highest level of scholarship attainable.

The coaching strategies, which have been used successfully in some of the most diverse classrooms in the United States, can help to:

- Empower individuals by allowing them ownership of their work,
- Improve organizational and note-taking skills,
- Overcome emotional and environmental challenges,
- Resolve conflicts,
- Ensure harmonious group or team work.

The teacher as coach has the determined objective of having students find their own way within a given structure. The teacher coach encourages students to attain the learning skills needed to move on to a higher level of achievement while realizing their academic potential (Kise 2006). It allows students to work freely within a given structure so that they become more independent and authentically produce work as it relates to the content studied (Crane 2002). This philosophy parallels Charlotte Danielson's Framework, which many states are using as a basis for teacher evaluation (The Danielson Group 2013).

As an example, the teacher as coach can employ the GOPER Model. Instead of telling the students what to do, they follow this simple structure: What is your **g**oal? What are your **o**ptions? Design your **p**lan of operation? Discuss ahead of time, how you **e**liminate your obstacles. Now, **r**eflect on how well you accomplished your goal. For a sample coaching strategy called the GOPER Model, please refer to the Digital Resource CD.

# How To Use This Book

## The Structure of the Simulations

*Active History: Civil War* includes five simulations.  Although each simulation stands alone, when completed together in sequence, students gain a strong understanding of the Civil War, its significance in American history, and how the concepts of the Civil War are relevant to conflicts today.

The first four simulations present scenarios where students are digging into the facts and circumstances of the Civil War.  The final simulation, Examining Conflicts Arising from Diversity, brings the context of the Civil War into more current times and has students identify a political conflict at the state or local level and debate the issue among the class.

## The Role of Essential and Guiding Questions

Essential and guiding questions support the implementation of the simulations provided in this resource.  The essential question is a defining one that serves as an umbrella for other guiding questions.  It helps to link concepts and principles and frames opportunities for higher-level thinking.  It is also so broad and open-ended that it cannot be answered in one sentence. To support the essential question, teachers should provide students with guiding questions. They relate to the big picture of the essential question but help narrow that question into its hierarchical components and often link subtopics together (Stix 2012).

In *Active History: Civil War*, there is one essential question that guides students to synthesize their understanding as a result of participating in all of the simulations.  Each simulation also includes up to four guiding questions to support the understanding of the essential question and probe students to think more deeply about the content.

# How To Use This Book *(cont.)*

## Objectives

The objectives provide a snapshot of the simulation and what students will be doing.

## Standards and Materials

Each simulation targets one McREL social studies content standard and two Common Core anchor standards. A list of necessary materials is provided for quick reference and planning/preparation.

## Questions

The overarching essential question and guiding questions are provided for easy reference throughout the lesson.

## Pacing Guide

A suggested schedule is provided to support planning and preparation for the simulation. This plan is a suggestion and can be modified in other ways to best fit your instructional time blocks. The lessons are divided into days.

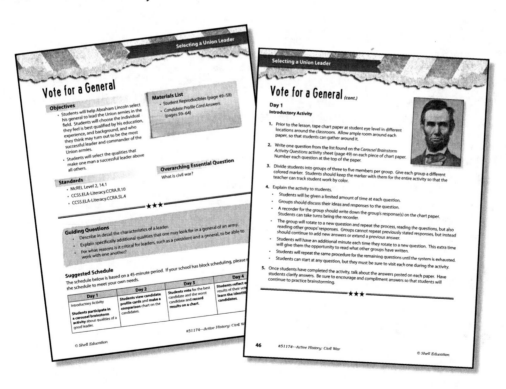

# How To Use This Book (cont.)

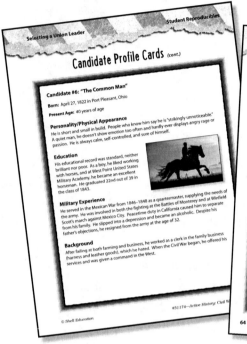

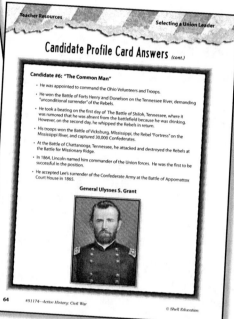

## Teacher Resources

A step-by-step lesson plan is provided to guide teachers and students through the simulation. As a guide, the lesson plan is broken down into sections by suggested days. Any necessary teacher or student resources are referenced throughout the lesson plan.

## Student Reproducibles

Any necessary student resources are provided at the end of each simulation lesson plan. These resources should be photocopied and provided to students throughout the course of the simulation. Resources include items such as planning guides, templates, rubrics, background-information pages, and graphic organizers.

## Digital Resource CD

All necessary student and teacher resources are provided on the Digital Resource CD. A complete list of the contents of the Digital Resource CD can be found on pages 134–135.

# Summaries of Simulations

## 1. Dred Scott Decision

In the first simulation, students be assigned one of four viewpoints on slavery and participate in a jigsaw discussion. Students familiarize themselves with each viewpoint by reading a letter or statement written by one of the following individuals:

Dred Scott, A Slave

Ellis Wilson, A Northerner

Marcus Thompson, A Southerner

J.F.A. Sanford, Abolitionist and New Owner of Dred Scott

## 2. Vote for a General

In the second simulation, students help Abraham Lincoln select a general to lead the Union Army during the Civil War. They choose the best individual for the job by analyzing résumés to determine which person possesses the best qualities to lead the Union.

**Candidates for General include:**

General George McCellan

General Joe Hooker

General Winfield Scott

General Ambrose Burnside

General Henry Wagner Halleck

General Ulysses S. Grant

## 3. Battle of Kaymat Simulation Game

In the third simulation, students simulate being a general who makes decisions at Kaymat (Gettysburg). The dispatch cards offer detailed information that helps students understand the complexities and consequences of war.

## 4. Civil War Fan Fold Designs

In the fourth simulation, students create fan fold designs based on the work of Yacov Agam. Students contrast perspectives of life before and after the Civil War. They discuss how the war affected lifestyle, social roles, rights, freedoms, and responsibilities of individuals in the North and South.

## 5. Examining Conflicts Arising from Diversity

In this final simulation, students examine how differing viewpoints that could lead to conflict, instead can instead be defused. Students are assigned a role, research a topic, and participate in a magnetic debate. They research the issues involved in the conflict and examine the viewpoints on those issues. Students reflect on their knowledge of conflict and the Civil War to form an opinion, take a stance, and engage in a public debate about the issues.

# Correlation to Standards

Shell Education is committed to producing educational materials that are research and standards based. In this effort, we have correlated all our products to the academic standards of all 50 United States, the District of Columbia, the Department of Defense Dependent Schools, and all Canadian provinces.

## How to Find Standards Correlations

To print a customized correlations report of this product for your state, visit our website at **http://www.shelleducation.com** and follow the on-screen directions. If you require assistance in printing correlations reports, please contact Customer Service at 1-800-858-7339.

## Purpose and Intent of Standards

Legislation mandates that all states adopt academic standards that identify the skills students will learn in kindergarten through grade twelve. Many states also have standards for pre-K. This same legislation sets requirements to ensure the standards are detailed and comprehensive.

Standards are designed to focus instruction and guide adoption of curricula. Standards are statements that describe the criteria necessary for students to meet specific academic goals. They define the knowledge, skills, and content students should acquire at each level. Standards are also used to develop standardized tests to evaluate students' academic progress.

Teachers are required to demonstrate how their lessons meet state standards. State standards are used in the development of all our products, so educators can be assured they meet the academic requirements of each state.

## McREL Compendium

We use the Mid-continent Research for Education and Learning (McREL) Compendium to create standards correlations. Each year, McREL analyzes state standards and revises the compendium. By following this procedure, McREL is able to produce a general compilation of national standards. Each lesson in this product is based on one or more McREL standards. The chart on page 16 lists each standard taught in this product and the page numbers for the corresponding lessons.

## TESOL and WIDA Standards

The lessons in this book promote English language development for English language learners. The standards listed on the Digital Resource CD support the language objectives presented throughout the lessons.

## Common Core State Standards

The texts in this book are aligned to the Common Core State Standards (CCSS). The standards correlation can be found on pages 15–16.

# Correlation to Standards *(cont.)*

## Correlation to Common Core State Standards

The lessons in this book are aligned to the Common Core State Standards (CCSS). Students who meet these standards develop the skills in reading that are the foundation for any creative and purposeful expression in language.

| Grade(s) | Standard | Page(s) |
|---|---|---|
| K–12 | **R.1** Read closely to determine what the text says explicitly and to make logical inferences from it; cite specific textual evidence when writing or speaking to support conclusions drawn from the text. | 20–24 66–69 124–127 |
| K–12 | **R.10** Read and comprehend complex literary and informational texts independently and proficiently. | 45–48 110–113 |
| K–12 | **W.4** Produce clear and coherent writing in which the development, organization, and style are appropriate to task, purpose, and audience. | 66–69 110–113 |
| K–12 | **SL.1** Prepare for and participate effectively in a range of conversations and collaborations with diverse partners, building on others' ideas and expressing their own clearly and persuasively. | 20–24 |
| K–12 | **SL.4** Present information, findings, and supporting evidence such that listeners can follow the line of reasoning and the organization, development, and style are appropriate to task, purpose, and audience. | 45–48 124–127 |

# Correlation to Standards *(cont.)*

## Correlation to McREL Standards

| Content | Standard | Page(s) |
|---|---|---|
| United States History | **14.1** Understands the technological, social, and strategic aspects of the Civil War (e.g., the impact of innovations in military technology; turning points of the war; leaders of the Confederacy and Union; conditions, characteristics, and armies of the Confederacy and Union; major areas of Civil War combat) | 45–48 |
| United States History | **14.3** Understands the impact of the Civil War on social and gender issues (e.g., the roles of women on the home front and on the battlefield; the human and material costs of the war; the degree to which the war united the nation; how it changed the lives of women, men, and children) | 66–69 110–113 |
| United States History | **13.2** Understands the development of sectional polarization and secession prior to the Civil War (e.g., how events after the Compromise of 1850 and the Dred Scott decision impacted sectional differences, southern justification for secession, the presidential leadership of Buchanan and Lincoln during the secession crisis) | 20–24 |
| Civics | **11.3** Knows major conflicts in American society that have arisen from diversity (e.g., North/South conflict; conflict about land, suffrage, and other rights of Native Americans; Catholic/ Protestant conflicts in the nineteenth century; conflict about civil rights of minorities and women; present day ethnic conflict in urban settings) | 124–127 |

# Background Information for the Teacher

In the 1850s, the United States was still a land of hope and promise. Most Americans were living well and comfortably, better than their parents before them, and with the expectation that if life was good for them, it would be even better for their children. In 1850, the nation was mostly rural, and while the growth of cities was steady and progressively continuous, farms, small towns, and villages dominated the demographics. The production of agricultural products was still worth more than the total output of the nation's factories and industries. There was an obvious energy throughout the nation, a palpable characteristic of what the American people had become and that would, in the short span of two decades, change the United States into the nation it is today. Many Americans of that generation would look back on this time with a degree of nostalgia, as if it were a "Golden Age," a time of peace and prosperity when everyone felt a serene contentment. The days were perceived as an idyll that others could only envy and wish for themselves. Yet this feeling of exhilaration could not contain the unraveling of this momentum, as the United States was becoming a nation divided by two separate and conflicting societies on a collision course.

Slavery was one of the factors that led to division between the North and the South. During the colonial era, slavery existed everywhere, but it was the South that became dependent on the system. Southerners needed cheap labor to work the tobacco, rice, and indigo plantations. In the North, especially during the years following independence, slavery gradually died out. Eli Whitney's invention of the cotton gin (cotton engine), a machine that could flawlessly separate the short fibers from the seeds, reinvigorated the agricultural economy and the slave system in the Southern states. Cotton became the major cash crop of the South. In 1800, the United States exported cotton valued at $5 million, or 7 percent of the nation's exports. By 1810, cotton exports were valued at $15 million, and in 1840, there were $63 million. By 1860, cotton would be 57 percent of the total exports of the United States with a value of $191 million. In the South, "Cotton was King," and it remained a static agricultural region where slavery became an institutionalized way of life.

The North was diametrically a region of growing cities and industries. Throughout the antebellum era, an industrial base was developing. Immigrants coming to the United States by the tens of thousands came to the North or else they headed out into the western territories. The Northern states were also rural and agricultural but with small holdings that relied on free labor.

Many Northerners began to take issue with slavery, seeing it as a degrading treatment of other human beings. Abolitionists throughout the free states openly condemned the southern states for their "peculiar institution," and as the criticism increased, so too did the South's determination to keep to its way of life. Southerners always feared that the day would come when the North would dominate politics and enact legislation that would abolish slavery and destroy their economy. It was easy for the abolitionists to speak out against slavery, but they did little to provide any solutions.

# Background Information for the Teacher (cont.)

The slave property in the South was worth as least two billion dollars the decade before the Civil War. If slaves could be confiscated or set free, how could it be done without ruining the Southern economy? Southerners objected to the high tariffs since they sold their cotton on the world market and wanted manufactured goods as cheaply as they could get them. There were many issues that led to discord, but they could have been settled amicably through the political process.

There was no agreement in sight over the issue of slavery. As tensions mounted, no compromise could be reached. The South was building a siege mentality, and they only saw Northern hostility and intransigence. John C. Calhoun had foreseen the day when the South would stand threatened by the overwhelming presence of the Northern free states and when the federal government itself would pose a threat to the Southerners' existence. The South believed it had a fundamental right to govern itself through states' rights, whereas the North believed in a federal government composed of unified states.

The Compromise of 1850 had held out the hope that somehow the irreconcilable differences would dissipate and that both sections could get on and bring about some understanding and a compatible coexistence. Those expectations came to a quick end when Northerners vowed to ignore and violate the Fugitive Slave Act, helping runaway slaves evade the pursuing posse and lawmen to get across into Canada and freedom. The formation of the Republican Party in 1854, a conglomeration of abolitionists, former Whigs, Free Soil, and anti-slavery Democrats, further exacerbated relations between the two sections. For the first time, Southerners were confronted by a political party that had its own political agenda that focused national attention on the issue of the abolition of slavery and threatened the Southern economy and political structure. Harriet Beecher Stowe's novel *Uncle Tom's Cabin* infuriated the South and did little to improve relations. The book sold 300,000 copies in its first year of publication. The Kansas-Nebraska Act and Stephen Douglas's suggestion that the territories be opened to "popular sovereignty," to let the people themselves decide the issue of slavery, raised an uproar in the North. Douglas got his transcontinental railroad, thanks to southern support, but opponents of slavery feared its spread into the territories and were not overjoyed. Kansas was eventually turned into a battlefield by both sides, and bloodshed and violence contaminated the issue that new states would either allow or prohibit slavery.

The Dred Scott decision in 1857, an effort to defuse the slavery issue and settle it once and for all, only served to make matters worse. Chief Justice Roger Taney and the Supreme Court ruled that Dred Scott should never have been allowed to bring suit since he was not a citizen. Furthermore, when the Supreme Court ruled that Congress did not have the power to exclude slavery from any of the territories, the North became enraged. Step by step, inexorably, the nation was moving toward disunion.

# Background Information for the Teacher *(cont.)*

The Lincoln-Douglas debates for the Illinois senate seat showed that Abraham Lincoln—with his "House Divided" speech—was no friend of the slave South and that Stephen Douglas could not be trusted. When John Brown attacked the federal arsenal at Harper's Ferry, hoping to ignite a slave insurrection throughout the Southern states, fear and panic took hold that the days of slavery were numbered. And finally, in the election of 1860, with Abraham Lincoln the Republican nominee making a run for the White House, the Southerners said "Enough," vowing to secede from the United States and sundering the Union if Lincoln was elected.

There had been high hopes that the 1850s would be a time for the sectional issues and differences to be settled amicably, but matters only seemed to deteriorate and get worse with each passing year. The petty political bickering, the sectional hatreds, and paranoid fears resulted not in agreement and peaceful settlement, but in conflict.

# The Dred Scott Decision

## Objectives

- Students will participate in a discussion involving whether or not Dred Scott should be freed.
- Students will take on the role of an abolitionist or an advocate of slavery during this time and plead their case.
- Students will utilize appropriate behavior and listening skills in order to reenact a public discussion.

## Materials List

- Reproducibles (pages 25–44)
- scrap paper
- pens or pencils

## Standards

- McREL United States History Level III, 13.2
- CCSS.ELA-Literacy.CCRA.R.1
- CCSS.ELA-Literacy.CCRA.SL.1

## Overarching Essential Question

What is civil war?

## Guiding Questions

- Economically speaking, the North and South have different ways of life. For what reasons was slavery considered vital to the South, much more so than to the North?
- In what ways did the differing sides justify their opposing viewpoints about the ethics of slavery before the Civil War?
- Describe in detail the role of an abolitionist.

## Suggested Schedule

The schedule below is based on a 45-minute period. If your school has block scheduling, please modify the schedule to meet your own needs.

| Day 1 | Day 2 | Day 3 | Day 4 | Day 5 | Day 6 |
|-------|-------|-------|-------|-------|-------|
| Introductory Activity<br><br>Students **learn about how slavery was affected** by different viewpoints. | Students **are assigned different viewpoints** regarding the Dred Scott case. | Students **write notes** about their specific viewpoints and **prepare for a discussion**. | Students **participate in a Stix Discussion**. | Students **write their ruling** and then **compare with what actually happened**. | Students **reflect on the discussion** with an assessment and then **discuss the guiding question**. |

# The Dred Scott Decision *(cont.)*

## Day 1

### Introductory Activity

1. Divide the class into four "expert" groups. Give each group a different page of the *Civil War Background Information* sheets (pages 25–28). Within each group, students should all have the same background information sheet.

2. Tell students to read the information as a group and then discuss the question at the bottom of the page. They should then write a thoughtful answer at the bottom of their pages. Inform them that they should read their text carefully. They will teach other groups as if they were "experts."

3. Give the groups time to prepare to share these thoughts with other groups.

4. Jigsaw the expert groups so there are students from all four groups present in the new groups that are formed.

5. Have students in the new jigsaw groups share their information and answers to the question in this order:
   - Colonial Background to Slavery
   - The Northern Way of Life
   - The Spread of Slavery from the South
   - The Start of the Civil War

6. As each jigsaw group shares, have students in the group who are listening complete the *How Slavery was Affected* sheet (page 29).

7. Close with a discussion and review what students learned by charting it on the board.

## Day 2

1. Read *The Dred Scott Case Background Information* sheet (page 30) aloud to the class to set the stage for this activity.

2. Distribute copies of the *Dred Scott, A Slave* sheets (pages 31–32) to the class and have students read it in small groups or with partners. Encourage students to annotate by underlining or highlighting parts that strike them the most. Allow students to talk about what they read.

3. Explain that the class will be participating in a discussion about the fate of Dred Scott. There will be four different perspectives, and each student will be assigned to represent one of these four perspectives.

# The Dred Scott Decision *(cont.)*

**4.** Divide the class into four groups and distribute a different perspective to each group. Two groups will represent the North and two groups will represent the South.

- *Ellis Wilson, A Northerner* (pages 33–34)
- *Marcus Thompson, A Southerner* (pages 35–36)
- *J. F. A. Sanford, Abolitionist and New Owner of Dred Scott* (pages 37–38)
- *A Slave Auctioneer's Letter to the Birmingham Sentinel* (pages 39–40)

**5.** Have students read these perspectives in their groups. Write the following questions on the board and have students discuss them together:

- Explain in detail your reaction to this passage.
- Even if you do or don't agree with it, for what reasons is this perspective important?
- Generate a list of what makes this perspective distinct, or different, from others.

## Day 3

**1.** Have students review the perspectives information they read in the previous class session regarding their assigned perspective.

**2.** Distribute the *Perspective Discussion Questions* sheets (pages 41–42) to students. Tell students to work individually or with partners to answer these questions about the perspectives.

**3.** Explain to students that they will be using these questions and answers to help them prepare for a discussion the following day, in which they will be sharing with others in the class who have different perspectives.

**4.** Have students share their answers to these questions in their groups, deciding on the best set of answers in preparation for the Stix Discussion the following day. Encourage students to know what they want to say and even practice for this discussion.

## Day 4

**1.** To prepare for the discussion, place one-third of the chairs in an inner circle. Behind each inner-circle chair, place a desk. Behind each desk, place two or three chairs. All chairs, in the inner and outer circle should be facing forward, toward the center of the circle. This will create an inner circle and an outer circle. Each letter in the diagram below signifies a different perspective. Be sure to have opposing sides face each other.

# The Dred Scott Decision *(cont.)*

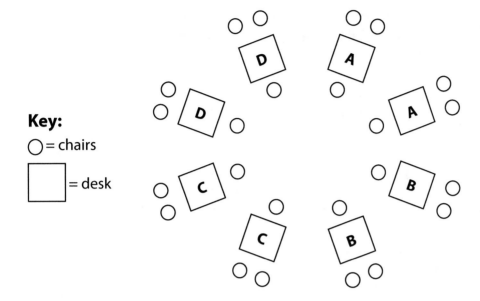

**Key:**

○ = chairs

☐ = desk

2. Place a small pile of scrap paper on top of each desk with pencils or pens.

3. Show students where to sit and how the diagram works. Check to ensure that the different viewpoints are seated in the correct places.

4. Explain to students that they will be part of a Stix Discussion, which is an inner-outer ring discussion. Students in the inner circle will discuss the issue, while in the outer circle, students serve as their clerks, feeding them information by passing notes. Tell clerks, or aides, that they are not allowed to pass a note while their member is actively speaking. They should wait until that person is finished speaking before tapping the shoulder and passing the note. Rotate the roles so everyone will have the opportunity to sit in the inner circle for the discussion.

5. Ask students to pretend they are the teacher who will be assessing their performance. The teacher embarks on the negotiable contracting of assessment with students. Generate a list of criteria that characterizes a good discussion from a weak one. Here is the criteria:

   a. Listening to a speaker and responding to what was said, instead of just talking for the sake of talking. Be sure to let them finish rather than interrupting them.

   b. To make your points more believable, use primary sources.

   c. Be courteous and respectful when making an argument.

   d. Give good eye contact and look at the person who is talking.

   Model the strategy for about two minutes. Tell students that it is a warm-up. Critique their performances so students have a clear understanding of their roles. Once you are satisfied, let the true discussion begin.

# The Dred Scott Decision *(cont.)*

6. Allow the inner circle a certain amount of time (five to seven minutes) for their discussion. Alert students when there is one minute left. When time runs out, rotate the students and allow the next group a turn in the inner circle. Be sure to give each group the same amount of discussion time.

## Day 5

1. Remind students of the main points brought out in the discussion the previous day. Tell students they must make a recommendation about the issue they discussed. As a group, they need to come to a consensus for their recommendation.

2. Have students form their groups again and generate as many ideas or solutions to the situation as possible. After their brainstorming session, tell the groups to rate their top five ideas by putting them in order from good to best. Call upon the groups to share their ideas and write each idea on the board.

3. Students will select from the items that were listed on the board to write a formal recommendation on their own paper. You can also have the class work together and write one formal recommendation on the board.

4. Discuss what actually took place historically the students by distributing copies of *The Ruling on Dred Scott* sheet (page 43). It is critical that you explain that there was no real "right or wrong" answer. With any decision, good and bad outcomes emerge.

5. On the T-chart provided on *The Ruling on Dred Scott* sheet (page 43), have students compare their ruling decisions with the actual ruling listed on their activity sheets.

## Day 6

1. To assess what students learned during this activity, distribute copies of the *Dred Scott Discussion Assessment* sheet (page 44) and have students respond to these questions either through a whole class discussion, small group discussion, or individually written answers.

2. Close the activity with a reflection on the guiding question for this lesson *In what ways did the differing sides justify their opposing viewpoints about the ethics of slavery before the Civil War?*

# Civil War Background Information 1

**Directions:** Read this background information in your group. Answer the question at the bottom of the page. Be prepared to share this background information and your answer with other groups.

## Colonial Background to Slavery

Slavery was present when Great Britain and King George III ruled the 13 colonies during the colonial period. In the southern colonies, farming was the most important way people made their living. The South had a long growing season and excellent soil. Much of the land was flat and leveled. It rained enough to keep the crops flourishing and watered. Cash crops like tobacco, rice, and indigo made many plantation owners rich. Later, cotton became the most important crop in the South. The people who owned the plantations believed that paying laborers to work on their lands was too expensive. If they paid people, they couldn't make profits. As a result, almost from the beginning, plantation owners began using slaves to work their land. During the 1700s and early 1800s, Blacks from the western coast of Africa and the West Indies made up a large part of the population in Maryland, Virginia, North and South Carolina, and Georgia.

When the 13 colonies rebelled against England, Thomas Jefferson wrote a declaration that would tell the world the reasons for America's revolution. At the Second Continental Congress in July 1776, the representatives discussed the words written by Jefferson. The statement "all men are created equal" was quickly accepted. In this passage, only white males were considered "men." The idea of abolishing slavery, mentioned elsewhere, was met with resistance. Some Southerners were not ready to give up the profits they were making through slave labor. In fact, these southern representatives said they would leave the meeting if the slavery statement was not taken out of the document. In the end, the line was taken out.

The United States became a nation that treated all men equally, except slaves. The differences and disagreements that the 13 colonies might have had about slavery were, for the time being, forgotten. The colonists had to win independence from England first before they could move forward as a nation, and they needed the unity of the 13 colonies to achieve this goal. The issue of slavery was momentarily put aside, but it would never really go away.

## Question:

Compare and contrast the definition of "all men are created equal" during the pre-Civil War period to today's standard.

_____

_____

_____

# Civil War Background Information 2

**Directions:** Read this background information with your group.  Answer the question at the bottom of the page.  Be prepared to share this background information and your answer with other groups.

### The Northern Way of Life

The idea of slavery never took hold in the North.  After the American Revolution, most of the northern states quickly abolished slavery.  The North was a section of the new nation where paying people for working was valued more than slave labor.  The northern states were developing industries (business) and building factories.  Cities were growing places for trade and commerce.  Farming was also important in the North, but farmers were able to make money even though they paid their hired hands and workers.  Immigrants were coming to the United States in bigger numbers.  Most of them lived in the growing cities of the North where they could find jobs.  Those who wanted to make a living from the land found many opportunities beyond the Appalachian Mountains, through the Ohio River Valley and on the prairie, and in the Far West.  Northerners wanted the federal government to make laws that would protect their growing industries.  They wanted a protective tariff to stop the importation of the cheap manufactured goods from Europe.  The northern businessmen were investing in growth and development.

## Question:

Generate at least 5 items that represented the growth of an industrial society in the North.

_____

_____

_____

_____

_____

# Civil War Background Information 3

**Directions:** Read this background information in your group.  Answer the question at the bottom of the page.  Be prepared to share this background information and your answer with other groups.

## The Spread of Slavery from the South

The South was a farming society.  It was agriculture that was at the heart of the southern economy.  Early on, Southerners developed the plantation system.  They grew tobacco, rice, and indigo.  Eli Whitney's cotton gin (a machine used for separating the fibers of the cotton from the seeds) made cotton profitable and ensured the growth of slavery.  Cotton production continued to increase every year.  The South grew millions of bales (large packs) of cotton to send to textile mills in Europe and the North.  By 1860, cotton represented 57 percent of America's exports and was valued at $191 million dollars.  The South had little industry (business activity), few major cities, and only a trickle of immigrants.  Southerners exported their cotton to the world markets and wanted to purchase cheap manufactured goods.  Southerners did not want the federal government to make laws that changed or harmed their way of life.

Slavery began to spread beyond the original slave-holding southern colonies as the United States acquired Louisiana and other western territories.  By the 1830s, Kentucky, Tennessee, Louisiana, Alabama, Mississippi, Florida, and Missouri were also slave states.  Some settlers in Texas—which gained independence from Mexico in 1836 and was annexed by the United States in 1845—were also pro-slavery.  Also at issue was whether slavery would be allowed in the Mexican Cession, the territories taken at the end of the Mexican-American War of 1846-1848.  Whenever new territories opened for American settlement, there were people who wanted to bring in slaves.  Conflicts occurred as these territories sought admission to the Union as states.  There was always confrontation about whether the states would be free states or slave states, since this determined how Congress would vote on legislation, and which section exerted greater influence in the federal government.

## Question:

Generate at least 5 items that represented the Southern lifestyle and need.

_____

_____

_____

_____

# Civil War Background Information 4

**Directions:** Read this background information in your group. Answer the question at the bottom of the page. Be prepared to share this background information and your answer with other groups.

## The Start of the Civil War

There were two very different ways of life in the two distinct sections of the nation. Factories and industries (businesses) were growing in the North. The South was mainly rural and depended on farming and plantation as a way of life. Southerners believed that slavery was needed for their profits and success. As abolitionists (people against slavery) in the North began to demand an end to slavery, the South felt threatened and under attack. The North grew more powerful as its cities, industries, and wealth grew. At this time, the Northerners' dislike of the slaveholding South also grew. When people could no longer calmly talk about the problems between the two sections, it seemed that war was the only answer.

Southern states threatened to secede (si-seed) (withdraw or break away) from the Union to form a new government if Abraham Lincoln was elected president. This was not the first time that such a threat was made. South Carolina and six other Deep South states viewed Lincoln's election victory as a threat to their way of life. South Carolina was the first state to secede from the United States.

Most people believe the Civil War was fought to get rid of slavery. There were many contributing factors to the Civil War. The differences between the North and South, such as values and ideas about society, the economy, industry, and slavery, were only part of the reason the Civil War was fought. Southerners wanted the extension of slavery into the territories. Many northern politicians resented the South's dominance in the federal government. They also wanted the Declaration of Independence to ring true that "all men are created equal"—whether white, black, brown, red, or yellow—to show the world that the United States was not a hypocrite. When the first shots were fired at Fort Sumter, Lincoln called for volunteers to end the rebellion. He was determined to keep the Union together. Lincoln told Southerners that they could keep their slaves as long as they remained in the Union. But it was too late. The time for calm discussion and compromise had passed. The South had decided to go its own way.

## Question:

The North and South had differing lifestyles. On a separate sheet of paper, compare and contrast how they differed on a T-chart. Write your answers below.

_____

_____

_____

# How Slavery Was Affected

**Directions:** As each group shares, write down a summary of how slavery was affected by the particular viewpoint and time in history.

| Civil War Background Information | Notable Points |
|---|---|
| Colonial Background to Slavery | _____ <br> _____ <br> _____ <br> _____ <br> _____ <br> _____ |
| The Northern Way of Life | _____ <br> _____ <br> _____ <br> _____ <br> _____ <br> _____ |
| The Spread of Slavery from the South | _____ <br> _____ <br> _____ <br> _____ <br> _____ <br> _____ |
| The Start of the Civil War | _____ <br> _____ <br> _____ <br> _____ <br> _____ <br> _____ |

# Dred Scott Case Background Information

Many of the problems that existed between the North and the South could have been solved without civil strife—even a volatile issue like the tariff was settled amicably—except the problem of slavery. The slave issue did not make allowance for reasonable discussion or compromise. The Compromise of 1850 was an agreement that was supposed to put an end to the disagreement over slavery. That ended very quickly when Northerners violated the agreement (the Fugitive Slave Act) and helped runaway slaves reach Canada and gain freedom. In 1854, the abolitionists (those against slavery)—free Soilers, former Whigs (supporters

of the American Revolution), and anti-slavery Democrats (those who believed in social equality) formed the Republican Party. The abolition of slavery was their main goal. The publication of Harriet Beecher Stowe's anti-slavery novel *Uncle Tom's Cabin* provoked bitter feelings and frustration in the South. Many events and incidents continued to pull the North and the South further apart.

The Dred Scott Supreme Court case in 1857 was heard in an effort to settle the slavery issue once and for all. Instead, the case only created more problems. Chief Justice Roger Taney and the Supreme Court had to decide whether or not Dred Scott should be allowed to sue in the courts, since as a slave, he was not considered a citizen of the United States. Furthermore, the Supreme Court's decision would ultimately affect whether Congress had the power to exclude slavery from the territories. This decade—the 1850s—was a time when the problems could have been resolved peacefully. Instead, it became a time when the United States drifted farther apart.

During the pre-Civil War years, the North and the South had the opportunity to work out the social, economic, and political differences that were causing the division between the two regions. The Dred Scott case was only one small factor that eventually led up to the Civil War. The new Republican Party, with its anti-slavery platform, was a threat to the South. In the mid-1850s, Abraham Lincoln emerged on the scene and became involved in national politics. The Lincoln-Douglas debates showed that Lincoln was no friend of the southern slaveholders. Lincoln and the Republicans were firmly opposed to the extension of slavery into the territories. Next, violence erupted in "Bleeding Kansas" to decide if it would be a "free" or "slave" state, which seemed to foreshadow the coming strife. In 1859, John Brown, a fervent abolitionist and fanatic, who believed slavery was an abomination and evil, attacked the United States government's arsenal at Harper's Ferry. John Brown wanted to spark a slave revolt throughout the South; he failed, was tried for treason, hanged, and became a martyr. Lincoln was elected president in 1860. At that point, South Carolina and other southern states seceded (left) from the Union. In 1861, the states that were once united under one government and one president were shattered by civil war.

# Dred Scott, A Slave

*Dred Scott was born into slavery. He never learned to read or write. His account of all that has happened and what led up to the court case is below:*

My name is Dred Scott. My mother was a slave, so I was born a slave. As soon as I could walk, I went to work in the fields. I probably picked more cotton, chopped more firewood, painted more fences, and fixed more carriage wheels than anyone around. My mother told me to obey my master, and if I did . . . everything would be fine. But mother always told me never to give up the hope of being free. She told me to have faith that someday there would be a Day of Jubilee, when all the slaves would be set free. My mother died with that hope in her heart. I never was a problem for anyone. I have never tried to run away. I have always lived with the hope that one day slavery would end. And I would be free at last.

I am very old now. As I get older, I do not see an end to slavery. I've lived my entire life as a slave, and all that time, I have never given up hope. Some of the southern people are nice, but some aren't. I've seen many slaves beaten. I've watched slaves whipped to the ground, their backs bloody. Many times I've seen slaves trying to run away, only to be tracked down by mean dogs and dragged back.

The auction block is a horrible place to see, as mothers and fathers are separated from each other and from their children. I know what it feels like to live in fear of being sold away from your family. I am now married to a free woman, and I have children of my own. We know we are lucky to be living together. But I am still a slave, and not one day goes by that we don't live with the fear of being separated. Every night we thank God for our good fortune—none of us has been sold, and we are still together as a family.

I'm telling you my story because I want freedom. The only way I can get freedom is from the courts. Remember, I'm old. I have worked hard all my life, and I don't have much time left. What little time I have, I want to be free. I want my family and me to move up North and live as free people. We want land. We want to work fields and make money. We want to sleep in our house, on our beds. We want to live in peace and freedom, far away from the world of fear and hatred. Living free means we won't have to worry about being sold and separated from each other.

# Dred Scott, A Slave (cont.)

I am weak. My back aches. My hair is gray. My bones are brittle. I'm no use to anyone as a slave. I can't work like I did when I was young. All I want now is freedom. My master made money selling the bales of cotton I picked. All I have is aches and pains all over my body. I'm just asking to be left alone and to live the rest of my days in freedom. I won't be a danger to anyone. I will go away quietly with my family.

I am seeking freedom through the courts because I lived on free soil. I know slavery is controversial. I know the abolitionists are angered by the spread of slavery into the territories. Many Southerners feel threatened. They want new lands for growing more cotton. I don't want to cause a problem. I would simply be very happy to be given my freedom. I feel I should be free because I once lived in a free state.

My master, Dr. Emerson (who's dead now), and I lived in Missouri, a slave state. But after we lived in Missouri for a while, Dr. Emerson took me to live in Illinois. Illinois is a free state. Dr. Emerson also took me to the Wisconsin and Minnesota Territories—also free areas. I am seeking freedom because I once lived in a state and territories that are free. It shouldn't make any difference that Dr. Emerson and I went back to Missouri. When I walked into Illinois, and the Wisconsin and Minnesota Territories . . . I earned my freedom.

Of course, Southerners will disagree with me. They say I am still a slave. They say that it doesn't matter if I live in a slave state or a free state. A slave is someone's property—no matter where he is taken or where he lives. Because I am seen as someone's property, my master can take me anywhere he chooses. No matter whether I am in a slave state or a free state, they believe I am still a slave.

I plead my case. I should be free because I was once on free soil. God help me gain my freedom.

# Ellis Wilson, A Northerner

At last, the day of reckoning has come.

The whole nation is waiting for the Supreme Court's ruling on the Dred Scott case. Both the North and the South want the issue clarified. We all know it goes beyond giving Dred Scott his freedom. Let the South keep their slaves, but they need to know that the North is determined to stop the spread of slavery into the territories. This case will determine the status of slavery. Once the court speaks, the course of the nation will be determined once and for all. All the attention that this case is getting is not just about one man. This case is about slavery itself. Can this nation finally hold up the Declaration of Independence so all the world can see that Americans truly believe "all men are created equal?"

The law says that Dred Scott is a slave. He was born in the slave state of Missouri. His mother was a slave. His owner, Dr. Emerson, once took him into the state of Illinois and then into the Wisconsin and Minnesota Territories. These are all free soil. Dred Scott rightly feels that he can sue for his freedom because of his residence in free territory. Even though Dr. Emerson eventually brought Dred Scott back to Missouri, his claim to be set free should be heard.

Of course, the South does not want a judgment in favor of Dred Scott. They do not want to see him gain his freedom through the courts. The Southerners fear his freedom would threaten their interests. They want to spread slavery as they seek more and more land to grow cotton. If Dred Scott's suit is successful, the Southerners think slaves throughout the South will plead for their freedom in court and win. In the back of every Southerner's mind is the constant fear of a revolt by the slaves. Plantation owners understand that a court outcome in favor of Dred Scott would put an end to slavery. They see the Dred Scott case as just another plot on the part of abolitionists (those against slavery) to create tension. They know their plantations can only survive as they do now with slave labor. They assume correctly that they will face economic ruin without their slaves. That is not a reason to keep a human being in bondage! The South must find a better way to safeguard its economy.

Southerners believe that because Dred Scott is a slave, he has no right to bring suit in the courts. He is simply property, and he does not have the same rights as a citizen of the United States. Slavery is not mentioned in the Constitution of the United States. Slaves are not even considered citizens under the Constitution. The South is outraged that the Dred Scott case has come this far and that the Supreme Court will decide the slave issue.

# Ellis Wilson, A Northerner (cont.)

The Southerners are frightened their civil rights will be violated by a decision in favor of Dred Scott. The South feels that if a master takes his slave to the North, to free soil, that the condition of the slave has not changed. The slave is still his (the owner's) property, just like a book, a piece of furniture, or a horse. The location of master and slave does not change the conditions of the master-slave relationship. Hopefully, Chief Justice Roger Taney and his associate justices will decide this issue once and for all. This will not be an easy issue to settle since taking a person's property must come through "due process," or legal fairness. This is guaranteed by the Bill of Rights. But isn't it time that this great nation of ours acknowledges that slaves are human beings? Slaves should not be regarded simply as someone's property. They have feelings, and they suffer pain just like you and I. This is not just about Dred Scott. It is about all slaves and whether we can go on as a nation that is half slave and half free. If it was only about Dred Scott, he would have been set free long ago. His youth is gone. He can barely stand up straight, let alone perform basic chores. He worked hard all his life, was obedient to his master, and never broke the rules that were set for him. He is a nice, and decent man, and he's a caring family man, too. He will not be a bother to anyone, and he should live his remaining years in peace and freedom.

We must set the minds of the Southerners at rest. We must make them understand that we do not want to take away their slaves. The North does not seek to dominate the South. But we also do not want to see the spread of slavery. There are limits to what the North will tolerate, and this is where the lines are drawn. This nation was founded on certain principles that were clearly set forth by Thomas Jefferson in the Declaration of Independence. It is unbearable that Americans are ridiculed by other nations for insisting that "all men are created equal" while Southerners keep slaves in bondage.

Dred Scott should be freed. He was brought to free soil. Having lived in free territory, he should be set free. If slavery is kept in the confines of the states that legally allow it, that is fine. The moment a slave is taken to free soil, the laws of that state or territory should apply. Eventually the South will learn and changes will come to their region as they did in the North. The Southerners will learn that slavery is an expensive burden. It is a hard lesson that the South will have to learn.

# Marcus Thompson, A Southerner

Vigilance, gentlemen, always vigilance. We must always stay alert! Vigilance today, vigilance now, and vigilance tomorrow.

The South must watch out for the dangers in front of us. The northern abolitionists are very determined. They will not be happy with anything short of destroying the slave system and our economy. My fellow Southerners must realize that we are in a struggle with people who will only be satisfied with our total defeat. The Republican Party has taken a firm stand against the further spread of slavery into the territories. They haven't even given thought to the needs of the planters and plantation owners who must seek fresh soil for the cultivation of cotton. Northerners are ready to believe any lies about the South. That horrible anti-slavery book by Harriet Beecher Stowe, *Uncle Tom's Cabin*, shows this to be true. Always ready to cause trouble, those abolitionists are urging a slave, Dred Scott, to bring suit in the courts to secure his freedom.

Dred Scott was born a slave. His whole life has been spent serving his master. What does Dred Scott know about freedom, and what will he do if he is set free? All Dred Scott knows is the kind hand of his master. A man who clothed, fed, and housed Scott for his whole life. If only God, in his majesty and wisdom, would help the North see what the South has accomplished with the slaves in their charge! Where would the slaves all go if they were set free? How would they all live? Left to themselves, they would either starve or become dependent on the goodwill and charity of others. The northern abolitionists do not consider the consequences of their actions. They just keep telling the slaves about the same ideas of freedom, over and over again. These Northerners have no clear idea about the future of these poor souls.

Dred Scott is no longer a young man. How will he be able to start a new life for himself? Here is a slave who was always treated well by his master, as is the case with most of the slaves. He is happy and content. He lives with his wife, Harriet. He is entering those years when he can finally enjoy a rest from all of life's labors.

This Dred Scott case is silly, and the North is behind the plotting. It is surprising that this suit has gotten as far as the Supreme Court of the United States. I, as a Southerner, question the right of Dred Scott to bring suit in the first place. Dred Scott is a slave. He is someone's property. He is not even considered a citizen of the United States! The Constitution of this great republic does not give Dred Scott recognition as a citizen; he had no right to bring suit in a court of law.

# Marcus Thompson, A Southerner (cont.)

Dred Scott was purchased by Dr. Emerson. It is common knowledge that when Dr. Emerson died, his widow wanted to set Dred Scott free. She could have set him free. Instead, Dred Scott became the tool of the abolitionists who urged him to bring suit in the courts, asking for his freedom. But we must now ask, if Dred Scott should be freed by the courts, how are the owners to be paid for their property? Again, we have an important issue that the abolitionists don't bother addressing.

Can the Supreme Court make a decision that will set Dred Scott free? Does the court have the power to deprive us of our property? Does Congress have that power as well? No! Property is protected by the Constitution and the Bill of Rights. All Americans are protected by due process. This means that every single slaveholder is entitled to a hearing before the government can take his property. If Congress dares to legislate an end to slavery, our rights are being violated. Let the northern abolitionists take a close look at the Constitution, which does not even address the issue of slavery. If I travel or move and decide to take my property with me, my ownership of my property does not change simply because I leave Alabama to go and live in Ohio. And so it is with Dred Scott. When master and slave went to live in Illinois, and afterwards to the Wisconsin and Minnesota Territories, the owner and slave relationship did not change. Could Dred Scott be taken away from Dr. Emerson any more than the book, the chair, the table, or the horse that he brought with him? Of course not!

Dred Scott is someone's property. He is not a citizen of the United States. He does not have the right to bring suit in the courts. Dred Scott and other slaves cannot be set free simply on the whim of Congress and the Supreme Court. That would deprive owners of due process. And the issue of compensation must be addressed. Before the South chooses to take action regarding Dred Scott, let us await the decision of Chief Justice Roger Taney and his associate justices. It may well be that the South has little to fear from this plot by northern abolitionists. Does the North really believe they treat their laborers and workers better than we do our slaves? Do they not see the poverty? Are they blind to the hunger in children's eyes? They conveniently look away from the crime, prostitution, below standard housing, unemployment, and poverty of their northern towns and cities. And still, they condemn us.

Let the North be warned that they can push the South only so far. Do not meddle with our way of life! We have given in too much already. We will not give the North our lives.

# J. F. A. Sanford, Abolitionist and New Owner of Dred Scott

Boldness is our answer. Always boldness. We live by our bravery and courage.

The South cannot be given a break from our attacks. We must fight the Southerners by making speeches, educating the politicians, and winning people to our side. The Supreme Court of the United States is deciding Dred Scott's suit. Here, we will strike another blow for freedom. We are determined to follow the path before us, and if we act boldly, we shall shake apart the practice of slavery. This is not the time to be timid.

Dred Scott belonged to my brother-in-law, Dr. Emerson. Missouri is a slave state, and that is where Dr. Emerson and Dred Scott lived most of their lives. My brother-in-law was an army doctor. He had to move around quite a bit. He once settled in Illinois and then stayed in the Wisconsin and Minnesota Territories. Dr. Emerson took Dred Scott with him on all these occasions. These trips to free soil are where the lawsuit has its strength. Abolitionists point out that since Dred Scott resided for a period of his life in a free state, where slavery is illegal, he should be granted his freedom. We realize there are other issues involved in this case, but it was worth pursuing if it helps our case and ends slavery. It doesn't really matter that the South considers Dred Scott's suit ridiculous. They argue that Dred Scott is a slave, and that by law, they can take their slaves wherever they please. They believe they can travel freely with their slaves in both slave and free states. The southern lawyers apply the "free state" status to permanent residents, not to people traveling through or residing temporarily in the area. Southerners also argue that they cannot be deprived of their property without due process. Southerners quickly quote the Constitution, hide behind the Bill of Rights, and demand due process. Yet, they never give a thought to how evil slavery is.

I have no patience with Southerners. I am a Yankee, born and raised in New York State. Just because I am an abolitionist doesn't simply mean I am against slavery. It means that I have dedicated my life to *end* slavery. I will do anything to end this terrible practice in the United States.

# J. F. A. Sanford, Abolitionist and New Owner of Dred Scott *(cont.)*

The abolitionists' cause is a holy cause. When Southerners use violence to attack slaves who wish to live on free soil, as they have in Kansas, then we must be prepared to fight back. If it takes a stern Christian like Reverend Henry Ward Beecher to lead the way, I will gladly follow. I have great faith in the power of the rifle to get the southern slaveholders to recognize that slavery is wrong. Many Northerners were upset when Beecher told abolitionists to ship rifles, not Bibles, to free soldiers fighting to bring Kansas into the Union as a free state. Like the Reverend Beecher, I believe that at this point, violence is the only way to get the Southerners' attention. The issue of slavery will only be solved by fighting.

The South threatens to break away from the Union every day. The South says it won't support federal laws. I say, let the South begin a war! They will regret their actions.

Many Northerners feel bad for the South. Many in the North do not agree with abolitionists. They are frightened that the freed slaves will take away their jobs. The South doesn't hesitate to use these fears against us. Some people in the North are mainly concerned about the spread of slavery into the new territories. Others believe slaves are not worth all this trouble. These people think the North should mind its own business. Abolitionists have been beaten by angry mobs. Some of our leaders have been hanged. These vicious (vish-*uhs*) attacks will not stop us from fighting for what we believe is right.

Abolitionists want the federal government to deal with these issues and decide what place slavery has in our society. I bought Dred Scott from Dr. Emerson's widow, who happens to be my sister. I pushed this suit through the courts to bring the issue to the attention of all people. I wanted to expose slavery as an institution that goes against American ideals of freedom. We have made our stand.

# A Slave Auctioneer's Letter to the *Birmingham Sentinel*

I am stunned. No, I am totally struck dumb.

My mind is numb. I could not believe the decision that has been made. I turn to you, my fellow citizens of this great state of Alabama, to tell me if what I heard and read about is true. The latest information is that the Supreme Court will hear Dred Scott's suit. Am I right? Is that what I read? Is that what I heard? Dred Scott, a slave, is actually bringing his suit all the way to the Supreme Court of the United States!

First of all, why is a non-citizen allowed to bring a suit into the courts? Secondly, what fools allowed all of this to go so far as the Supreme Court? And finally, is Chief Justice Roger Taney crazy for even considering hearing the suit in the first place? Chief Justice Taney and his court could have said they would not hear the suit and that would have been the end of it.

The northern abolitionists say Dred Scott's suit is legal and well within the law. Well, gentlemen, if that is the law, then the law is a joke. Do I have to remind everyone that Dred Scott is a slave? He was born a slave, and he will die a slave. He is not a legal citizen of the United States. He is not a citizen because he is simply the *property* of the individual who paid for him on the auction block. Since he is legally considered property, he does not enjoy the same rights that are granted to you and me under our Constitution. This very same document makes no mention of slaves and slavery. The issue of slavery was a matter that was left to each individual state to decide for itself. As this system now exists, Dred Scott is not a citizen. He has no rights and should never have been allowed to bring this lawsuit before the courts.

The abolitionists will give us no peace. They are a danger to the entire South. They encourage trouble in our communities with their calling for an end to slavery. They are a mob that breaks the law. They help runaways and refuse to return the slaves to their owners under the provisions of the Fugitive Slave Act. They will lie about the South, so they can destroy our agricultural (farming) society and use any means and every method to do it.

# A Slave Auctioneer's Letter to the Birmingham Sentinel (cont.)

I am personally insulted when my friends and I are faced with accusations of cruelty and inhumanity. The business firm of Throttle & Whimple performs a valuable service to the whole southern community in supplying the labor needs of the plantations. All of the workers' needs are met with as much compassion and understanding as circumstances allow. We, who bring a much-needed service to all of our neighbors throughout the South, do so with dignity. We offer planters and plantation owners the opportunity to choose the workers and the staff they need to help them live a comfortable southern lifestyle. Northerners tell lies that slaves are beaten and that families are forcibly broken apart and sent away. None of this bothers me in the least. I hold my head up with pride that I am a valuable member of the South's trade and commerce. Who tells these lies? Where do these wild rumors start? Ask these questions, and in reply, you'll always find one answer: *the northern abolitionists*. They always lie. They quote anti-slave novels like *Uncle Tom's Cabin*, which are the made-up ravings of a woman. Or they publish trash like William Lloyd Garrison's *The Liberator* that lies about events and tells its readers that it is news. Be warned! Our dear South is being attacked by villains (vil-*uh*ns) who want to hurt us.

As a southern gentleman, I don't go and accuse those in the North of treating their workers poorly and ignoring the problems of the weak and needy. Do I criticize the North for all the misery that poisons their industries? The northern factories and mills are filled with weakened bodies. The workers labor long hours for low pay, seven days a week, in terrible conditions. The factories are dangerous, as the horrible conditions cripple the men, women, and children who are the helpless victims of greed. These enemies speak with such innocence. If you compare the two, is slavery so terrible? Remember the words of our dear Savior, "Let him who be without sin cast the first stone." Am I, a slave dealer and auctioneer, more terrible than the greedy industrialist? Is there more blood on my hands than on his? Is my heart of stone and his is not? I think not. I believe God in heaven would agree.

**Submitted by Roland Throttle, Esq. on October 4, 1857**

**Throttle & Whimple, Auctioneers, Birmingham, Alabama**

# Perspective Discussion Questions

**Directions:** Write your assigned perspective on the line provided. The questions below will help you bring up important points during the discussion. Answer these questions from the point of view of your assigned perspective in the Dred Scott case.

**Perspective:** _____

1. Describe specifically whether your sympathies (feelings of support and loyalty) lie with the southern slaveholders or with the northern abolitionists.

   _____

   _____

   _____

2. For what reasons is your perspective important?

   _____

   _____

   _____

   _____

3. List the main points you are trying to express through your perspective.

   _____

   _____

   _____

4. List primary sources or artifacts you could use to make your argument stronger.

   _____

   _____

   _____

# Perspective Discussion Questions *(cont.)*

**5.** From the opposing side's perspective, list at least three things you have to prepare yourself for and how you would prepare your answer.

_____

_____

_____

_____

_____

_____

**6.** Describe specifically what you want the verdict of the case to be.

_____

_____

_____

_____

_____

**7.** In what ways will you persuade people to take your side?

_____

_____

_____

_____

_____

_____

# The Ruling on Dred Scott

**Directions:** Below are the points in the ruling on the Dred Scott case. Compare your ruling to these in the space below.

> **a.** The Supreme Court ruled against Dred Scott.
>
> **b.** It ruled that his temporary stay on free soil (free territory) had not made him a free man.
>
> **c.** The court ruled that Dred Scott did not have the right to bring suit since he was not a citizen.
>
> **d.** Most importantly, the court stated that Congress did not have the right or the power to prohibit slavery in the territories.
>
> **e.** The court ruled that the Missouri Compromise of 1820, prohibiting slavery in parts of the Louisiana Territory, was unconstitutional.
>
> **f.** The court could not take away a person's property without the due process of the law, which is protected under the Fifth Amendment of the Bill of Rights.

| **My Ruling Decisions** | **Actual Ruling Decisions** |
|---|---|
|  |  |

# Dred Scott Discussion Assessment

**Directions:** These questions are specific to the historical background on the case. Think about your own opinions for each of these questions. Then, respond based on what you think, not what your assigned perspective might think.

1.  For what reasons was or wasn't Dred Scott a citizen of the United States?

    _____

    _____

2.  Explain specifically whether or not he had the right to bring suit to the federal courts.

    _____

    _____

3.  If you were traveling to a foreign country today, as a visitor, do you think their local laws should apply to all individuals, or just the ones who reside there? With this understanding, for what reasons did or didn't living on free soil (free territory) make Dred Scott a free man?

    _____

    _____

4.  In what ways was the Missouri Compromise of 1820 constitutional?

    _____

    _____

5.  For what reasons does or doesn't Congress have the power to determine if a territory should allow slavery or be free?

    _____

    _____

# Vote for a General

## Objectives

- Students will help Abraham Lincoln select his general to lead the Union armies in the field. Students will choose the individual they feel is best qualified by his education, experience, and background, as well as they think may turn out to be the most successful leader and commander of the Union armies.

- Students will select the qualities that make one man a successful leader above all others.

## Materials List

- Reproducibles (page 49–58, 65)
- Teacher Resources (pages 59–64)
- chart paper

## Standards

- McREL United States History Level II, 14.1
- CCSS.ELA-Literacy.CCRA.R.10
- CCSS.ELA-Literacy.CCRA.SL.4

## Overarching Essential Question

What is civil war?

## Guiding Questions

- Describe in detail the characteristics of a leader.
- Explain specifically additional qualities that one may look for in a general of an army.
- For what reasons is it critical for leaders, such as a president and a general, to be able to work with one another?

## Suggested Schedule

The schedule below is based on a 45-minute period. If your school has block scheduling, please modify the schedule to meet your own needs.

| Day 1 | Day 2 | Day 3 | Day 4 |
|-------|-------|-------|-------|
| Introductory Activity<br><br>**Students participate in a carousel brainstorm activity** about qualities of a good leader. | **Students view candidate profile cards** and **make a comparison** chart on the candidates. | **Students vote** for the best candidate and the worst candidate and **record results on a chart**. | **Students reflect on** the results of their vote and **learn the identities of the candidates**. |

# Vote for a General (cont.)

## Day 1
### Introductory Activity

1. Prior to the lesson, tape chart paper at student eye level in different locations around the classroom. Allow ample room around each paper, so students can gather around it.

2. Write one question from the list found on the *Carousel Brainstorm Activity Questions* sheet (page 49) on each piece of chart paper. Number each question at the top of the paper.

3. Divide class into groups of three to five members per group. Give each group a different colored marker. Students should keep the marker with them for the entire activity so their work can be tracked by color.

4. Explain the activity to students.
   - Students will be given a limited amount of time at each question.
   - Groups should discuss their ideas and responses to the question.
   - A recorder for the group should write down the group's response(s) on the chart paper. Students can take turns being the recorder.
   - The group will rotate to a new question and repeat the process. They will read the questions but also read other groups' responses. Groups cannot repeat previously stated responses, but instead should continue to add new answers or extend a previous answer.
   - Students will have an additional minute each time they rotate to a new question. This extra time will give them the opportunity to read what other groups have written.
   - Students will repeat the same procedure for the remaining questions until the system is exhausted.
   - Students can start at any question, but they must be sure to visit each one during the activity.

5. Once students have completed the activity, discuss the answers posted on each paper. Have students clarify answers. Be sure to encourage and compliment answers so students will continue to practice brainstorming.

# Vote for a General *(cont.)*

## Day 2

1. Tell students an important historical decision needs to be made and *they* are going to help make it. Tell them President Lincoln needs to fill the position of Union general. He needs students' advice.

2. Ask students to individually write down a list of qualifications they would like to see in a candidate for the position. They should think about the carousel brainstorm activity from the previous lesson.

3. Have each student share his or her qualifications in small groups. Have the groups make a final list of qualifications they would like to see in candidates for the position. Let the groups share their lists with the class.

4. Distribute copies of the *Candidate Profile Cards* sheets (pages 50–55) to students. Within their groups, have students read the candidate profiles. Remind students to think about the lesson's guiding questions.

5. Tell students to compare and contrast the information about the unnamed candidates using the *Candidate Comparison Chart* (page 56).

## Day 3

1. Remind the class of the candidate profile cards. Give them time to review the cards and talk about a decision for the best candidate in their groups.

2. Once the group decides on the individual whom they think would be the best and most successful in the position, have them record their reasons for this selection in writing on the *Vote for a General Questions* sheet (page 57).

3. Have the groups decide on the individual whom they think would make the poorest choice for general. Have students explain and justify their decisions on the *Vote for a General Questions* sheet (page 57).

4. Take a vote from the class and create bar graphs for the most-favored and the least-favored candidates. You can distribute copies of the *Vote for a General Results Chart* (page 58) to have students create individual graphs.

5. Examining the bar graph, tell the class you will now discuss each individual candidate.

6. Call out "Candidate #1," and ask all students to turn to that candidate's profile card. Groups who favored each candidate tell the class the reasons why. If time permits, this can be followed by groups who liked him the least. The discussion should consider whether education, leadership, ethics, etc., were factors in their decision-making process.

# Vote for a General *(cont.)*

7.  Display the first candidate's sheet from the *Candidate Profile Card Answers* (pages 59–64). If possible, reveal each line separately as you move from the top to the bottom of the page to prevent students from seeing the actual name found at the bottom of the card. This way, students will listen to the achievements or disappointments of each person before they hear the name.

8.  Discuss Candidate #2, and then reveal the answer to Candidate #2, and so on.

## Day 4

1.  Read the background of what really happened on the *What Really Happened?* sheet (page 65).

2.  Pose the following questions to the class and have students talk to a partner about it: *After hearing what actually happened to the candidates in real life, describe in detail what you have learned from this activity. In what ways were you surprised by the outcome of the simulation?*

3.  Assess what students understand by having them write a reflection using the following questions: *In what ways were or weren't you surprised by Lincoln's decision? For what reasons aren't people hired solely by their resume? For what reasons is it vital to meet someone one-on-one?*

# Carousel Brainstorm Activity Questions

## Part 1

**Directions:** Answer the questions below as a warm-up before participating in carousel brainstorming.

1. Generate a list of as many leaders you can think of (in school, or on a local or national level).

## Part 2

**Directions:** Answer the questions below as part of your carousel brainstorming.

1. What is the number one quality a good leader should have?

2. What kind of job experiences should a good leader have?

3. Who is the worst leader from history? Explain in detail your reasoning.

4. Describe in detail the kind of life experiences a good leader should have.

5. How much education does a good leader need?

6. Generate a list of the worst qualities a leader could have.

# Candidate Profile Cards

## Candidate #1: "The Young Napoleon"

**Born:** December 3, 1826 in Philadelphia, Pennsylvania

**Present Age:** 36 years of age

### Personality/Physical Appearance

He is not very tall, yet he always looks like a soldier. He is considered to be a go-getter and looks like he would be able to do any job. He often disagrees with his superior officers. He is very sure of his abilities and not willing to compromise. He sometimes twists the truth and even believes some of his own made up stories. He makes some people feel unimportant.

### Education

He was admitted to the University of Pennsylvania at the age of 13, and he entered West Point United States Military Academy at the age of 15. He was a member of the Dialectic Society—the smartest of the West Point upperclassmen. He graduated from West Point second in his class in 1846.

### Military Experience

He was acknowledged for bravery in the Mexican War with Winfield Scott at the taking of Mexico City. He served on a special military committee in Europe to study the military. While abroad, he studied European armies and wrote about what he observed. When the South seceded (left the Union), he was made a general of the Ohio troops and won West Virginia for the Union, scoring a minor military victory.

### Background

He left the army in 1856 and worked for the railroads as a manager.

# Candidate Profile Cards *(cont.)*

## Candidate #2: "A Fighter"

**Born:** 1814 in Massachusetts

**Present Age:** 48 years of age

### Personality/Physical Appearance

He has a military style, especially on horseback, when reviewing his troops. He is not married. While serving in the Peacetime Army in California, there was a rumor that he drank and gambled. He enjoys parties with friends. He has a big mouth and brags a lot. He is often sorry and regrets what he says.

### Education

He graduated from West Point United States Military Academy, ranking 29th of 50 students in 1837. Many people reported he was a brilliant student, but his behavior was bad and pulled him down in ranking.

### Military Experience

He fought in the Mexican War from 1846–1848. During the war, he was rewarded three times for courage and bravery on the battlefield. He was Chief-of-Staff to five different generals, and he managed their commands, gaining a wide range of experience. He left the army in 1853.

### Background

Congress made him a brigadier general (in command of a brigade or troop) when the Civil War broke out. He served bravely in every major battle in the early months. He fought and won more battles than any other general during his 16-month leadership.

# Candidate Profile Cards (cont.)

## Candidate #3: "The Loyal Southerner"

**Born:** 1786 in Petersburg, Virginia

**Present Age:** 76 years of age

### Personality/Physical Appearance

He is six feet, five inches in height and weighs over 300 pounds. He is very religious. He is called "Old Fuss and Feathers" because he likes wearing gold braids on his uniform. He is strict and conceited (snotty and arrogant). He is a tea drinker and has never consumed alcoholic beverages.

### Education

He briefly attended the College of William and Mary in Virginia. When the United States and England were close to war in 1807, he gave up his law studies to join the army.

### Military Experience

In 1810, he was a captain of the artillery (weapons unit). During the War of 1812, he was a brigadier general (in command of a brigade or troop), scoring a great victory at the Battle of Chippewa (CHIP-*uh*-wah) in 1814. Severely wounded, he emerged as a hero from the British stalemate at the Battle of Lundy's Lane near Niagara Falls. In 1841, he was named General of the United States Army. In the Mexican-American War of 1846–48, he landed at Vera Cruz in 1847, his forces defeated and took control of Mexico City after many battles.

### Background

In 1852, he ran for president for the Whig Party, but he lost the election to Franklin Pierce. He was the first soldier since George Washington to hold the rank of lieutenant (loo-TEN-*uh*nt) general.

# Candidate Profile Cards *(cont.)*

### Candidate #4: "Handsome Sideburns"

**Born:** May 23, 1824 in Liberty, Indiana

**Present Age:** 38 years of age

## Personality/Physical Appearance

He is handsome, big, and brawny (six feet tall and broad shouldered). He is thought of as a top soldier. A brave, gallant soldier and true patriot, he is considered honest, trusting, and good humored.

## Education

For his early education, he was privately tutored by Samuel Bigger, a future governor of Indiana. He attended West Point United States Military Academy, excelled in mathematics, and graduated 18th out of a class of 38 in 1847. He chose artillery (weaponry) as his branch of service.

## Military Experience

He was commissioned a second lieutenant (loo-TEN-*uh*nt) in the Third United States Artillery. In 1847, he was on active duty in Mexico but didn't see any combat. In 1849, he served in the Indian Wars against the Apache in New Mexico. In 1851, he was made a first lieutenant in the U.S. Army. He resigned from the army in 1853.

## Background

He opened a business in 1853, the Bristol Rifle Works, in Bristol, Rhode Island. He invented a well-made, but expensive gun. In 1857, he lost all of his money and then got a job with Illinois Central Railroad as branch treasurer (a person responsible for handling money). By 1860, he had managed to pay off all his old bills.

# Candidate Profile Cards (cont.)

## Candidate #5: "Old Brains"

**Born:** 1815 in New York

**Present Age:** 47 years of age

### Personality/Physical Appearance

He is a talented manager and good at paperwork. His knowledge of strategy and how to fight a war is excellent, but he lacks the desire to make aggressive war.

### Education

He graduated from West Point United States Military Academy in 1839 and served in the army for 15 years. While in the army, he wrote the book *Elements of Military Art and Science* in 1846.

### Military Experience

A highly educated soldier, he was a headquarters operator who could handle all of the regular chores very well. In 1861, he was given command of the Missouri Department of War. After the Battle of Shiloh, he took command of the Western Army of approximately 100,000 men and divided them into smaller groups. He waited and moved too slowly, throwing away the chance to defeat the Rebels.

### Background

He resigned from the army in 1854. He became a lawyer in California and helped develop the state's constitution. He returned to the military at the beginning of the war.

# Candidate Profile Cards (cont.)

## Candidate #6: "The Common Man"

**Born:** April 27, 1822 in Port Pleasant, Ohio

**Present Age:** 40 years of age

### Personality/Physical Appearance

He is short and small in build. People who know him say he is "strikingly unnoticeable." A quiet man, he doesn't show emotion too often and hardly ever displays angry rage or passion. He is always calm, self-controlled, and sure of himself.

### Education

His educational record was standard, neither brilliant nor poor. As a boy, he liked working with horses, and at West Point United States Military Academy, he became an excellent horseman. He graduated 22nd out of 39 in the class of 1843.

### Military Experience

He served in the Mexican War from 1846–1848 as a quartermaster, supplying the needs of the army. He was involved in both the fighting at the Battles of Monterey and at Winfield Scott's march against Mexico City. Peacetime duty in California caused him to separate from his family. He slipped into a depression and became an alcoholic. Despite his father's objections, he resigned from the army at the age of 32.

### Background

After failing at both farming and business, he worked as a clerk in the family business (harness and leather goods), which he hated. When the Civil War began, he offered his services and was given a command in the West.

# Candidate Comparison Chart

**Directions:** Use the chart below to compare the candidates as you view the profile cards.

| Candidate's Name | Unique Viewpoint He Could Give to the Civil War | Strengths | Weaknesses |
|---|---|---|---|
| # 1:<br><br>The Young Napolean | | | |
| # 2:<br><br>The fighter | | | |
| # 3:<br><br>The Loyal Southerner | | | |
| # 4:<br><br>Handsome Sideburns | | | |
| # 5:<br><br>Old Brains | | | |
| # 6:<br><br>The Common Man | | | |

# Vote for a General Questions

**Directions:** Answer the questions below.

**1.** Describe in detail the qualities you would look for in a general.

_____

_____

_____

_____

_____

_____

**2.** Who is your favorite choice for general?  Describe in detail your reasons for choosing this man.

_____

_____

_____

_____

_____

_____

_____

_____

# Vote for a General Results Chart

**Favorite Candidate**

| Number of Votes | #1 The Young Napoleon | #2 A Fighter | #3 The Loyal Southerner | #4 Handsome Sideburns | #5 Old Brains | #6 The Common Man |
|---|---|---|---|---|---|---|
| 10 | | | | | | |
| 9 | | | | | | |
| 8 | | | | | | |
| 7 | | | | | | |
| 6 | | | | | | |
| 5 | | | | | | |
| 4 | | | | | | |
| 3 | | | | | | |
| 2 | | | | | | |
| 1 | | | | | | |
| 0 | | | | | | |

**Candidate Name and Number**

# Candidate Profile Card Answers

**Candidate #1: "The Young Napoleon"**

- He attacked Richmond, but in the famous Seven Days' Battles, he was forced to retreat by Robert E. Lee.

- He was relieved (fired) of his command by President Lincoln after Antietam because he moved so slowly and wouldn't advance against Lee.

- He always thought he was outnumbered by the Confederates, when in reality, he had the bigger army and the advantage.

- In 1864, he was the Democratic candidate for the presidency. He lost to Lincoln. Some of his former soldiers even voted against him.

- After the war, he was elected governor of New Jersey on two occasions.

- He returned to being an executive for the railroads.

### General George McClellan

# Candidate Profile Card Answers (cont.)

### Candidate #2: "A Fighter"

- He strongly stated that the nation needed a dictator to win the Civil War. This did not make President Lincoln happy, but Lincoln gave this man a leadership position despite his remarks.

- In a surprise maneuver, he attacked General Lee from behind at Chancellorsville. Lee attacked back, causing this general to lose faith in himself and his plan.

- He was relieved (fired) of his command three days before Gettysburg for not moving against Lee.

- The city of Boston honored him with a statue.

### General Joe Hooker

# Candidate Profile Card Answers *(cont.)*

### Candidate #3: "The Loyal Southerner"

- He was a living military hero of the War of 1812 and the Mexican War.

- He advised President Lincoln and his cabinet to have patience and prepare carefully for the Civil War. His advice was ignored, and the North went into shock after their defeat at the First Battle of Bull Run.

- He created the "Anaconda Plan" (named after the Anaconda snake, which strangles its prey) to strangle the South by blockade and capture the Mississippi River Valley. He believed the South could be starved into surrender.

- He remained general only during the first year of the war. He resigned his post in 1862.

- He retired to West Point United States Military Academy and died two years later.

**General Winfield Scott**

# Candidate Profile Card Answers *(cont.)*

### Candidate #4: "Handsome Sideburns"

- He did not want to lead the Army of the Potomac, and he initially turned President Lincoln down. He accepted the post the second time he was asked but stated that he was not qualified.

- To attack the Rebels, he ordered his men to charge up a hill at Fredericksburg. He lost 12,000 men in just a few hours.

- His officers revolted against him during the famous "Mud March," and Lincoln relieved (fired) him of his command.

- Lincoln had him serve in a lesser post. He fumbled an attack at Petersburg and was once again relieved of his post.

- He returned to private life and business, but he gave his name to the fancy style of whiskers called "sideburns."

### General Ambrose Burnside

# Candidate Profile Card Answers *(cont.)*

**Candidate #5: "Old Brains"**

- He was a good administrator, but his advice on strategy was muddled (confusing) and unclear.

- In July 1862, he was appointed to an administrative position (office or business management) to get him away from the front lines where his lack of experience caused problems for his men.

- As commander in chief, his skill in training soldiers contributed to the success of other leaders under his command.

- He was not respected by other generals and was very unpopular.

- President Lincoln named him Chief of Staff in 1864. He held that position until the end of the war.

**General Henry Wagner Halleck**

# Candidate Profile Card Answers *(cont.)*

### Candidate #6: "The Common Man"

- He was appointed to command the Ohio Volunteers and Troops.

- He won the Battle of Forts Henry and Donelson on the Tennessee River, demanding "unconditional surrender" of the Rebels.

- He took a beating on the first day of The Battle of Shiloh, Tennessee, where it was rumored that he was absent from the battlefield because he was drinking. However, on the second day, he whipped the Rebels in return.

- His troops won the Battle of Vicksburg, MIssissippi, the Rebel "Fortress" on the Mississippi River, and captured 30,000 Confederates.

- At the Battle of Chattanooga, Tennessee, he attacked and destroyed the Rebels at the Battle for Missionary Ridge.

- In 1864, Lincoln named him commander of the Union forces. He was the first to be successful in the position.

- He accepted Lee's surrender of the Confederate Army at the Battle of Appomattox Court House in 1865.

### General Ulysses S. Grant

# What Really Happened?

**Directions:** Read the background information and reflect on the questions at the bottom of the page.

President Lincoln clearly saw the need for full-scale war, but his generals did not. George McClellan continually dragged his feet and had to be prodded (poked or encouraged) into action. Lincoln said the man suffered from the "slows"—and he was being kind when he said it. General McClellan created a great army, trained it well, and saw that the men had the best equipment to take into battle. Unfortunately, McClellan didn't know how to effectively use that army. General Ambrose Burnside was a poor choice for overall command of an army. Burnside himself knew it and turned down the command when it was first offered. Lincoln and the nation found out Burnside didn't quite fit the bill after the Battle of Fredericksburg, where 12,000 men fell in just a few hours. Even "Fighting Joe" Hooker was not the man for the job. After the Battle of Chancellorsville, when Lee moved north into Pennsylvania, Hooker wanted to attack Richmond instead of Lee's army. General Meade also disappointed Lincoln. At the Battle of Gettysburg, when the fighting was finished after Pickett's Charge, General Meade hesitated and did not advance against General Lee on the heights of Seminary Ridge to defeat the Rebels. Lincoln was disappointed because he knew Lee would get away and continue the fight. Lee did fight for another two years.

For close to three years, Lincoln could not find a commander who would fight the war the way it had to be fought. McClellan was fired. Burnside and Hooker were relieved (fired) of the overall command. Even Meade, as good as he was at Gettysburg in holding his own against Lee's army, was not given the top slot. These were West Point United States Military Academy graduates. They served in the Mexican War and had résumés that were perfect. On paper they looked good, but in action, they left much to be desired.

In March of 1864, Abraham Lincoln finally decided on his man. Grant was considered a failure in everything he tried to do. Not only did he fail at farming and business, but he was regarded as an alcoholic by many people who knew him. Early in the war, after the second day at the Battle of Shiloh, he pushed the Rebels back and won the day. Those close to Lincoln advised that Grant should be fired. They accused him of being away from the battlefield and said that he had been drinking. To that Lincoln replied, "I cannot afford to lose him. He fights." Lincoln knew Grant was a fighter. Grant persevered at Shiloh, took Vicksburg, and greatly defeated the Rebel Army of Tennessee at the Battle of Chattanooga. Soon after, he was named general of all the Union armies. Grant went east and took command. He attacked Lee in the spring of 1864 and continued to attack until he destroyed the Rebel army.

Grant was a genius for waging war. He also had the nerve, character, disposition, and personality to send men into battle to die.

**Reflection Question:** After hearing what actually happened to the candidates in real life, what have you learned from this activity? In what ways were you surprised by the outcome of the simulation?

# Battle of Kaymat Simulation Game

## Objectives

- Students will become exposed to the ugliness of war, the horror of pain and suffering, and the destruction of many lives as they reenact the Civil War battle.
- Students will take on the roles of generals and make the same decisions, which affected the fates of soldiers fighting in the battles, during the simulation.

## Standards

- McREL United States History Level II, 14.3
- CCSS.ELA-Literacy.CCRA.R.1
- CCSS.ELA-Litearcy.CCRA.W.4

## Materials List

- Reproducibles (pages 70–109)
- *Battle of Kaymat Spinner* (page 77) reproduced on cardstock
- construction paper
- scissors
- cardstock
- brass brads
- hole punchers
- spinners
- plastic chips

## Overarching Essential Question

- What is civil war?

## Guiding Questions

- For what reasons can an internal conflict, such as a civil war, be so harsh on families who may be fighting on opposite sides?
- Explain specifically the emotional and physical challenges that soldiers faced while engaged in battle.
- Generals often had to decide the fates of many human beings. In what ways did this affect their battle strategies?

## Suggested Schedule

The schedule below is based on a 45-minute period. If your school has block scheduling, please modify the schedule to meet your own needs.

| Day 1 | Day 2 | Day 3 | Day 4 | Day 5 | Day 6 | Day 7 |
|---|---|---|---|---|---|---|
| Introductory Activity<br><br>Students **participate in a vocabulary activity** and **read** background information. | Students **learn how to play the Battle of Kaymat game** and **begin playing**. | Students **continue to play** the **Battle of Kaymat game** and then **reflect** on the varied viewpoints of the battle. | Students **continue to play** the **Battle of Kaymat game** and then **reflect** on the varied viewpoints of the battle. | Students **continue to play** the **Battle of Kaymat game** and then **reflect** on the varied viewpoints of the battle. | Students **continue to play** the **Battle of Kaymat game** and then **reflect** on the varied viewpoints of the battle. | Students **finish playing** the **Battle of Kaymat game** and then **close with a reflection** on the varied viewpoints of the battle. |

# Battle of Kaymat Simulation Game *(cont.)*

## Day 1
### Introductory Activity

1. Have students look over the vocabulary words and definitions found on the *Battle Vocabulary Cards* sheets (pages 70–71) for a few minutes, or assign it for homework the night before this lesson. Place the words on a word wall in the classroom.

2. Make copies of the *Battle Vocabulary Cards* sheets (pages 70–71) and cut them apart. Each student will secretly be assigned one word. Tape one word to every student's back without that student seeing his or her word.

3. Tell students they will be playing a game called *Vocabulary Identity Crisis* with their classmates.

4. To play, each student will find a partner who will give one clue about the word. The student will try to guess his or her word using the clue. Once the student guesses that word, he or she must use it correctly in a sentence. If the student needs another clue, he or she must find a different partner to give another clue. This repeats until the student has guessed the word correctly and used it correctly in a sentence.

5. Students should take turns guessing words and giving clues until everyone has guessed his or her word.

6. End the lesson by having students read the *Battle of Kaymat Background Information* sheets (pages 72–73).

# Battle of Kaymat Simulation Game *(cont.)*

## Day 2

1. Place students into groups of four, and within each group, assign two students to the Union and two to the Confederates. Students should locate the headquarters of the leader of their side. The Confederate leader is General Robert E. Lee, and the Union leader is General George Meade.

2. Make copies of the *Battle of Kaymat Map* (page 74) game board at 200% or larger, and distribute one map to each group. Explain that the *Battle of Kaymat Map with Markers* sheet (page 75) shows a bird's-eye view of the battlefield. Students will be asked to examine the map from that bird's-eye perspective to locate the different areas that will be discussed in the simulation.

3. Make game pieces using circles cut from construction paper or purchasing chips. Explain that all Confederate game pieces will be labeled with the letter *C* and all Union game pieces will each be labeled with the letter *U*.

4. Using the *Battle of Kaymat Map Key* (page 76) as a reference, have students locate the following features on the maps by pointing to them.
   - Roads: Chambersburg Pike, Fairfield Road, Emmitsburg Road, Taneytown Road, Baltimore Pike, Hanover Road, and York Pike
   - Hills: Culp's Hill, Little Round Top, and Big Round Top
   - Trostle Farm, the wheat field, the peach orchard, and Devil's Den
   - Cemetery Ridge and Seminary Ridge
   - Rock Creek and Plum Run Creek
   - Town of Kaymat

5. Distribute the chips and a *Battle of Kaymat Spinner* (page 77) (reproduced on cardstock or can be easily purchased on the Internet) to each group as well as copies of the *How to Play the Game* sheet (page 78), and read through it as a class. Have students put together their spinners. As students play the game, you will need to distribute the corresponding pages found in the *Battle of Kaymat Dispatches and Spin Cards* sheets (pages 79–99) and *Generals' Decisions of Action* sheets (pages 101–105). Have students cut out cards. Groups will also need copies of the *Soldier Fate Sheet* (page 100).

6. Have students set up their game boards and begin to play the game.

7. During the last 10 minutes of class time, ask one of the questions found on the *Whole-Class Discussion Questions* sheets (pages 106–109). These questions pose situations where the students have to decide what they would do in the place of one of the characters in the situation and give students great insight into what the lives of the people of Kaymat were like during the battle.

# Battle of Kaymat Simulation Game (cont.)

## Days 3–6

1. Continue playing the game.

2. You will need to distribute the corresponding pages found in the *Battle of Kaymat Dispatches and Spin Cards* sheets (pages 79–99) and *Generals' Decisions of Action* sheets (pages 101–105).

3. During the last 10 minutes of class time, ask one of the questions found on the *Whole-Class Discussion Questions* sheets (pages 106–109).

## Day 7

1. If students have not finished the game, they should finish at the beginning of class.

2. Ask one of the questions found on the *Whole-Class Discussion Questions* sheets (pages 106–109).

3. Reveal that this battle was actually named the Battle of Gettysburg, not Kaymat. Allow students to share what they know about Gettysburg. Students read Abraham Lincoln's Gettysburg Address because it is one of the most important speeches ever made historically. Questions such as the following could be posed:

   • Describe in detail how Abraham Lincoln's address healed the wounds of a divided nation.

   • Generate a list of the points that make this speech so great in your opinion.

   • If you were the president, explain in your own words how this battle affected you emotionally.

4. End the lesson with a discussion about one of the guiding questions listed in the beginning of this unit:

   • For what reasons can an internal conflict, such as a civil war, be so harsh on families when family members find themselves on opposing sides? (It could even be brother against brother, and father against a son!)

   • In what ways were local towns affected as battles were sometimes fought in one's backyard?

   • Posters and advertisements always portray soldiers looking clean, neat, and heroic. Describe in detail the realities of what it was like to engage in battle.

   • Explain specifically the emotional and physical challenges that soldiers faced while engaged in battle.

   • Generals often had to decide the fates of many human beings. In what ways does this affect their battle strategies?

# Battle Vocabulary Cards

| | |
|---|---|
| **bayonet**<br><br>a blade that attaches to the muzzle of a rifle; used for stabbing in close combat | **corps** (kohr)<br><br>a military unit led by a lieutenant general; usually consisting of three divisions and one artillery (weapons) brigade/battalion (troop) |
| **Rebel**<br><br>a Confederate soldier from the South | **musket**<br><br>a long-barreled shoulder gun with a smooth opening (not as accurate as the modern rifle) |
| **brigade**<br><br>a military unit led by a brigadier general, usually consisting of four to six regiments, or battle groups | **Confederacy**<br><br>a union of states or group of people who share a common cause or goal; also known as the Confederate States of America, these seven Southern states all seceded (left) from the Union |
| **cannon**<br><br>this weapon is a large bronze or iron barrel (tube) mounted on a carriage drawn by horses that fires deadly projectiles (i.e., round shot [a large metal ball of many distinct weights and sizes], or canister [casings or cylinders filled with small projectiles, pellets, or lead bullets]) that are loaded through the muzzle | **regiment**<br><br>a military unit led by a colonel, usually consisting of 10 companies, or groups of men |

# Battle Vocabulary Cards *(cont.)*

| | |
|---|---|
| **Union**<br>made up of the states of the United States that did not secede (leave) to form the Confederacy; the government set up in 1861 by seven southern slave states | **canister**<br>a metal cylinder fired from a cannon that burst and scattered deadly pellets |
| **division**<br>a military unit led by a major general or a brigadier general, usually consisting of three to five brigades, or troops of men | **federal**<br>the central authority that governs and is made up of united states |
| **general**<br>a military officer who can command a brigade, division, corps (kohr), or the whole army | **cavalry**<br>military troops that fight on horseback |
| **Yankee**<br>a supporter of the Union, or states that did not believe in slavery | **commander**<br>an officer in command of a military unit or troop |

# Battle of Kaymat Background Information

## Why Study the Battle of Kaymat

The Battle at Kaymat took place in July of 1863. The battle lasted three days. It is still one of the greatest land battles ever fought in North America. It is thought to be the bloodiest battle in our nation's history. Antientam is still considered the bloodiest day in American history, when 25,000 Americans were killed and wounded. During the three days of fighting at Kaymat, however, over 50,000 men were killed and wounded. No other battles in all of the wars we have fought as a nation have been bloodier.

## The Second Invasion of the North

The South wasn't successful at the Battle of Antietam during General Robert E. Lee's first invasion of the North in 1862. As a result, in 1863, Lee decided to attempt to invade the North again. In the spring of 1863, Confederate General Lee won his most brilliant victory at Chancellorsville, Virginia. He smashed and defeated a Union army that was twice as big as his army of Northern Virginia. At the end of June, with his army numbering more than 79,000 men, Lee decided to invade the North. Lee thought the war needed to be brought to the northern states. Virginia had been torn apart and destroyed by the fighting for the past two years. Now Lee and Confederate President Jefferson Davis wanted to give the Northerners a taste of real war. Lee's army marched north through the Shenandoah (shen-*uh*n-DOH-*uh*) Valley. They were shielded from the Union Army by the mountains. His cavalry troops were commanded by General J. E. B. Stuart. Stuart was sent to stir up trouble behind the Union lines and to keep Lee posted about the Union Army's movements. Lee's army moved fast across the Potomac and through Maryland into northern territory even before the Union Army and Abraham Lincoln realized what was happening. Lee broke his army into smaller parts, and they invaded large areas of the countryside, gathering food and supplies from the farmers, towns, and communities. The Confederate soldiers were dressed in rags and had bare feet. They were hungry and eager to take whatever they could from the countryside.

## The Road to Kaymat

The Union Army knew Lee was invading the North. They began to move north to stop him. The Union leaders did not know exactly where Lee was. Lee also knew nothing about the movements of the Union Army because Stuart was far away making his own raids on the countryside. Stuart had not reported anything to his commanding officer. Lee began to worry. He didn't know where the Yanks (the Union Army of the Potomac) were, his army was in bits and pieces, and he was afraid of being attacked. He took out a map and studied it carefully. He decided to send messengers to all of his commanders to come back together at Kaymat. His army was spread out across the region, but all the roads led to this small town. Lee decided to gather his army back together there. The new commander of the Union Army, General George Meade, sent out his First Corps (kohr) to find the Rebels (the Confederate Army of Northern Virginia). They also made their way toward Kaymat because the many roads located there would make it easy for them to find Lee's army.

# Battle of Kaymat Background Information *(cont.)*

## The First Day of the Battle

On the first day of July, Union soldiers on the northern edge of Kaymat met a small group of Rebels marching toward the town. The first shots that were fired by both sides alerted other Confederate and Union forces. Soldiers from all over began to run towards the sound of gunfire. None of the commanders actually meant to fight a battle. However, once the first shots were fired and other soldiers arrived, a battle had begun. Soon, messengers were sent to both General Lee and General Meade.

Commanders placed the Union soldiers of the First Corps on the heights north of Kaymat, but the rest of the Union Army was too far away to be much help. Lee's army was much closer. The Rebels pushed the Yankee lines back. Lee's troops fought the whole day through the streets of Kaymat, pushing the Yanks out of the town. The Yanks pulled back to the high ground southeast of Kaymat. As night began to fall, the Rebels held their positions and waited for the rest of their army to come together. At the same time, the Union soldiers waited for General Meade to arrive with the rest of their troops.

## Preparation for the Next Day's Battle

That night, the Union soldiers dug in south of the town. The Rebels took positions opposite the Union lines, and they, too, waited for morning and the rest of their army. General Lee and his men gained a major victory on that first day at Kaymat, but they didn't destroy the Yanks. Now, Lee had some hard decisions to make. They were on enemy territory. When the next day dawned, they had to decide what action to take. *They* were the invaders. *They* could retreat and make a good getaway, or they could attack. But whether they retreated or attacked, *they* had to take the first step. General Meade knew that he could sit, wait, and hold his defensive positions as long as he wanted. Lee had to move. He had already gathered in as much as he could over this wide area, and food and supplies for his men would be hard to find. He couldn't afford to stay in one place too long. Lee made his decision, and on the second day, he put his plan into action.

## Getting Started with the Simulation

To begin, you and your group will create a mini-skit, setting the stage for the main battle that took place on Days II and III. In class, you will be acting out the last two days of the battle by moving pawns on a battle map. The map you will be using will show the positions of the Rebels and the Yanks on the morning of the second day of the Battle at Kaymat. You will participate in a simulation of this battle. You will not change the outcome, but you will see what happened on that battlefield and why it happened. While playing the simulation, you will read dispatch cards, spin for the fate of your fellow soldiers, and research questions for class discussion. Through playing this game, you will better understand why the Battle of Kaymat was such a terrible and unforgettable experience for more than 170,000 Americans.

# Battle of Kaymat Map

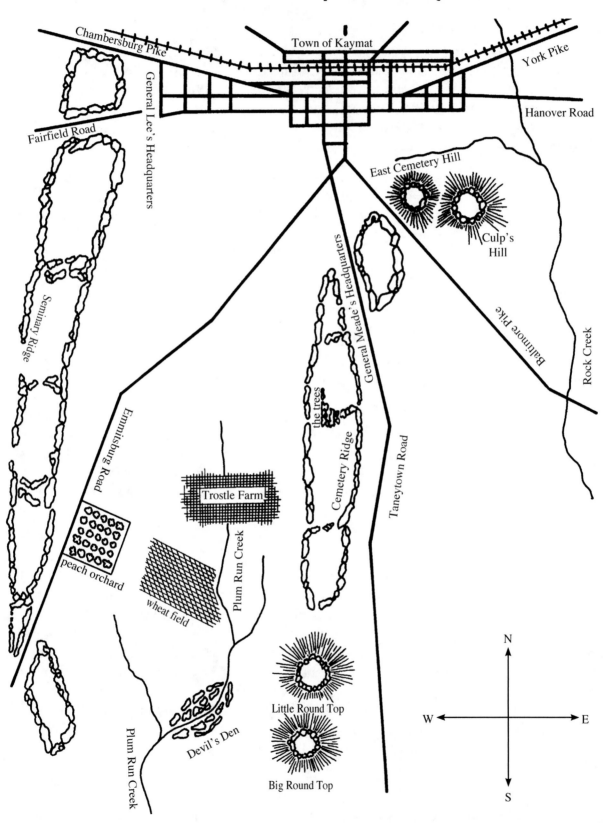

# Battle of Kaymat Map with Markers

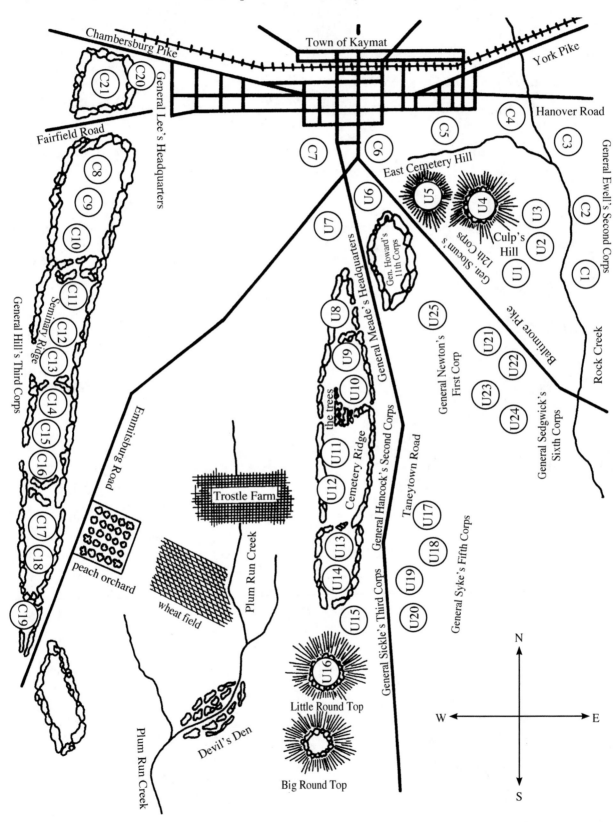

# Battle of Kaymat Map Key

hill =

railroad =

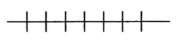

creek =

streets in town =

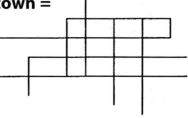

pikes/roads =

large ridges =

Confederate troops = **C**

Union troops = **U**

compass =

N

W ← → E

S

peach orchard =

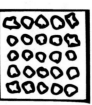

wheat field =

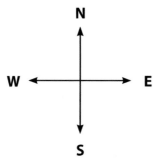

farm =

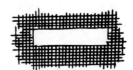

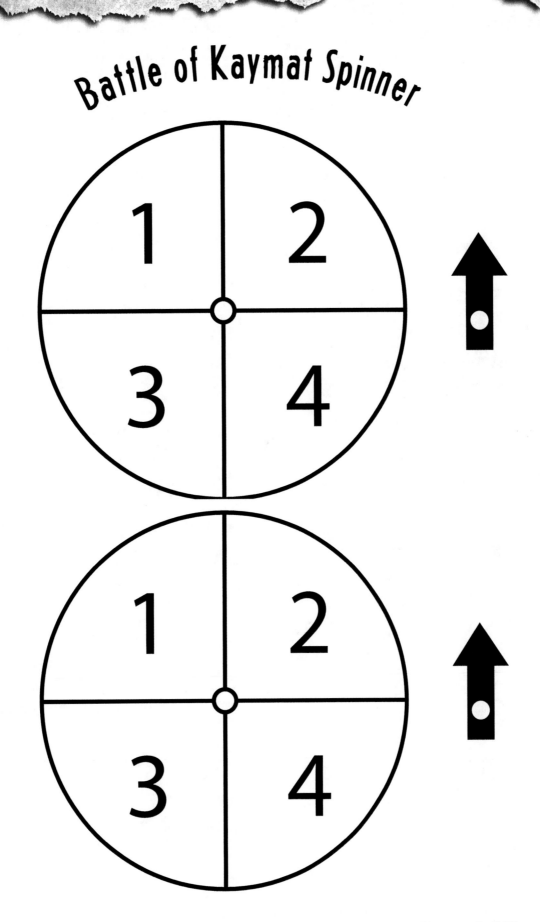

Battle of Kaymat Spinner

# How to Play the Game

**Directions:** Follow the steps on this page to set up and play the game.

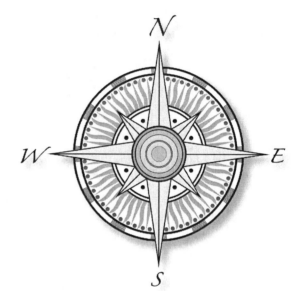

1.  Label each side or edge of your map with the cardinal directions using the compass on the lower right side of the map: north, south, east, and west.

2.  Put together your spinner.

3.  Each chip is marked with specific identification so you will know where to place it on the board. Use the *Battle of Kaymat Map with Markers* sheet (page 75) as a reference while setting up the initial board.

4.  Your group will take turns reading the 16 dispatch newspaper reports written by a reporter who witnessed the battle on the *Battle of Kaymat Dispatches and Spin Cards* sheet (pages 79–99). The italicized text will tell your group how to move the pieces on the map. Your teacher will give these to you.

5.  Stop every three cards to complete a *Generals' Decisions of Action* sheets (page 101–105).

6.  After reading each dispatch card, one person from each side has the opportunity to spin to determine the fate of one of his or her comrades, or buddies. The spin section is located below each dispatch card. You will see two names written on top of that spin section, one for each side. The names of the soldiers are real. However, your group may alter history as you are now responsible for determining the soldier's fate with a spin.

7.  After spinning and reading the results of the spin, students from each side will check off the fate of their fellow soldier on the *Soldier Fate Sheet* (page 100).

8.  Work with partners to offer your opinions of what you would have done if you were in a similar situation. Respond to the situation from the point of view of the general from the side for which you are representing.

9.  Once you have set up your simulation pieces on the game board, discuss the following questions within your group:

    a.  By observing the pieces on the map, describe which army you believe is larger.

    b.  Which army do you think has the advantage at the start of the second day? Describe in detail how you have come to this conclusion.

# Battle of Kaymat Dispatches and Spin Cards

## Dispatch #1

### General Dan Sickles's Blunders

In the early morning hours of July 2, General Meade starts to pull his army together. Parts of the Union Army are still scattered. They begin to establish their battle line along Cemetery Ridge, with the right side on Culp's Hill and the left side on the Round Tops. *(Point to Cemetery Ridge.)*

Meade places General Sickles and the Third Corps (kohr) *(U13 through U16)* on his left. They extend south from the end of Cemetery Ridge, where the high ground starts to level off, all the way to the Little and Big Round Tops. General Sickles is worried he will be attacked in a weak position if he remains where he was placed by General Meade. In the course of the day, he pushes out to the Emmitsburg Road, into the peach orchard and wheat field. *(Move chips U13 through U16 forward of the Union lines over Plum Run Creek. Move U13 and U14 just inside the peach orchard. Move U15 and U16 onto the wheat field.)*

No one will ever call into question the personal bravery of General Sickles. But by day's end, there are serious doubts as to his sanity, judgment, and common sense. By moving so far forward, General Sickles opens a gap in the Union line and places the Third Corps in an exposed and dangerous place.

When General Meade makes a personal inspection and discovers the Third Corps is out beyond the Union lines, he is horrified. The rumble of cannon signals the beginning of General Longstreet's attack, and Meade realizes it is too late to do anything but fight. *(Show the opening action by moving chips C15 through C19 slightly forward towards the peach orchard and wheat field on three sides, in the direction of the Third Corps chips—U13 through U16. No contact is made yet.)*

# Battle of Kaymat Dispatches and Spin Cards *(cont.)*

## Spin Card #1

**Union soldier:** *Henry Kendrick*
**Confederate soldier:** *Bryan Grimes*

**If you spin a 1:** As a scout, he is sent to feel out the enemy positions. He hears the rumbling of cannons and hurries back to the safety of his own lines. His last thought is of home as the sharpshooter's bullet hits him squarely in the back and passes through his heart.

**If you spin a 2:** He helps establish a front line, but he's fired upon by the enemy and driven back to his own position. Two of his friends are brought down by enemy fire. He is unharmed.

**If you spin a 3:** While scouting, he spots enemy movement. He starts to pull back, and he's wounded in the exchange of fire. He returns to his regiment with a flesh wound, but by day's end, he is told he is fit to go back into the battle.

**If you spin a 4:** Together with several other soldiers, he advances to the front line. He makes his way towards the enemy. A cavalry soldier on horseback rides him down. He's captured and made a prisoner.

# Battle of Kaymat Dispatches and Spin Cards (cont.)

## Dispatch #2

### Longstreet's Attack

General Longstreet's men, led by General Hood and General McLaws, swarm into the peach orchard and the wheat field and attack the Union soldiers. Within minutes, all is in an uproar. The Union Third Corps (kohr) battle lines simply melt away as men begin to panic and retreat from the battle to a place of safety.

The Rebel divisions *(C15 through C19)* attack the Union soldiers *(U13 through U16)* from three sides. The swiftness of the attack is frightening. Above the crashing sounds of battle, the horrifying Rebel yell can be heard.

What remains of the Third Corps (those not killed, wounded, or taken prisoner) retreat across Plum Run Creek into Devil's Den. *(Show this by moving U13 through U16 back towards Devil's Den. Move C15 through C19 forward, through, and on both sides of the wheat field. Since Sickles lost many of his men, either killed, wounded, or taken prisoner—remove U15 from the board entirely.)*

It is here and around the Round Tops that the fighting will seesaw back and forth throughout the late evening and into the night. Both sides will go at each other with bullet, knife, bayonet, rocks, and fists.

## Spin Card #2

**Union soldier:** *John Irvin*

**Confederate soldier:** *Charles Phelps*

**If you spin a 1:** The first explosion of gunfire pours into his ranks as the attack begins. A bullet smashes into his thigh and shatters his leg. He lies under the broiling sun until night. Then doctors finally take him to a field hospital where his leg is cut off.

**If you spin a 2:** In the first rush, as the battle lines clash, he's clubbed in the head and knocked down. His head is soaked with blood, but he recovers after several minutes and rejoins his unit.

**If you spin a 3:** The position he holds is momentarily overrun, and he's made a prisoner. He is quickly taken behind the fighting lines with other men who were captured.

**If you spin a 4:** The first firing of the cannon is a roar that shatters the silence and stillness of the hot day. Half of the men in his army outfit (military group) panic. They run to the rear areas, scared out of their wits. He cries tears of shame. Eventually he makes his way back to the regiment and puts his fear behind him.

# Battle of Kaymat Dispatches and Spin Cards (cont.)

## Dispatch #3

### General Warren and the Round Tops

General Warren is sent by General Meade to check out the left side of the Union line. The two hills at the extreme left of the Union line, Little and Big Round Tops, are supposed to be held by General Sickles and the Third Corps (kohr). He scouts Little Round Top and finds it completely deserted by Federal troops.

General Warren quickly orders troops from Sykes' Fifth Corps up to the high point of Little Round Top. Other soldiers are put in place on Big Round Top. Warren personally oversees the movement of a line of cannons to the top of this high ground. *(Move U20 to the top of the Big Round Top. Move U19 to the top of Little Round Top. Move U18 into U15's original space.)*

A regiment from Maine, commanded by Joshua Chamberlain, is told to hold Little Round Top at all costs. The troops and guns are all in place in the nick of time. Soon, the first Rebel soldiers begin to emerge from Devil's Den. The Rebels start heading towards the Union troops.

*(Move U13, U14, and U16 in the eastern direction to the bottom of Little Round Top. Move C17 through C19 up into the base of Little Round Top, touching the Union chips on the west side.)*

## Spin Card #3

**Union soldier:** *Charles Reed*
**Confederate soldier:** *William Pender*

**If you spin a 1:** An exploding cannon shell shatters several trees and a large wooden splinter is driven into his hip. He is knocked out from the pain, but doctors find him. He's moved to a field hospital. He survives the surgery.

**If you spin a 2:** The battle lines of the Rebels and the Union soldiers crash together. All he remembers is the flash from a rifle just a few feet away. His arm is shattered by a bullet and has to be cut off. He goes into shock and dies on the operating table.

**If you spin a 3:** The men in his regiment form their battle line and open a deadly fire at the enemy. All he can remember is the constant loading and reloading of his musket rifle and the deafening noise. By day's end, he is totally exhausted but unharmed.

**If you spin a 4:** The men in his outfit, or military group, scatter into Devil's Den. Everyone finds a place behind barriers of rocks and logs. He survives the battle into the darkness of night, and makes his way back to his regiment.

# Battle of Kaymat Dispatches and Spin Cards *(cont.)*

## Dispatch #4

### General Sykes's Fifth Corps to the Rescue

As the attack of General Longstreet's Rebels sweeps the Third Corps aside, a cannon ball takes off General Sickles's right leg. He is carried off the battlefield on a stretcher, calmly smoking a cigar. The developing disaster on the Union left is dealt with by giving orders to General Sykes to move the Fifth Corps forward to fill the gaps in the Union line. Brigades and regiments of the Fifth Corps march double-time and move rapidly towards the sound of the guns. *(Move U17 into U13's original position to help the beaten troops running from the field.)*

The fighting that is taking place at Kaymat is spread out over several square miles, and the continuous crash of the cannon sounds like the rolling thunder of a severe summer storm. Everywhere in the heat and humid air of this July day is a covering of smoke that hangs and drifts across the fields, ridges, and distant hills. It is very difficult to see.

Only flashes, like lightning, reveal the firing of cannons. Longstreet sends some of his divisions into the gap between the Third Corps and the Round Tops. *(Move C15 and C16 in front of U14's original position, as this is a gap in the Union line.)* The screams of dying horses are shrill and horrible to hear. They mix with the moans of the wounded men who litter the field.

Seeing the approach of the Rebels, Sykes's Fifth Corps moves quickly and begins to fill the gap in the Union line, which at the moment, stops Longstreet's attack. *(Move U18 North into U14's original position. Move U13 into U15's original position. This spreads the troops throughout this area, from the Round Tops to the southern tip of Cemetery Ridge. Now push C15 and C16 back across Plum Run Creek northwest of Devil's Den.)*

# Battle of Kaymat Dispatches and Spin Cards *(cont.)*

## Spin Card #4

**Union soldier:** *Jacob Click*

**Confederate soldier:** *James Dearing*

**If you spin a 1:** The regiment charges across the field and into the guns.  A blast of canister from a cannon leaves 20 men around him on the ground, but he's untouched.  He continues to advance with what's left of the men from his regiment.

**If you spin a 2:** The blast from a cannon picks him up and carries him back several feet.  It knocks him to the ground, shattering his leg with pellets.  He's carried to the surgeon who has to cut his leg off.  He survives the operation.

**If you spin a 3:** The charge moves his entire brigade across the field.  The soldier who carries the flag falls, and he grabs the banner to lead the men into the guns.  He is the first to break into the enemy line, surprisingly untouched, alive without a scratch.

**If you spin a 4:** He only remembers the feeling of his lungs wanting to burst from the effort of running across the open field.  Then, he sees a flash from the mouth of a cannon.  He feels his body carried backward by the searing blast.  He dies within moments.

# Battle of Kaymat Dispatches and Spin Cards *(cont.)*

### Dispatch #5

### The Minnesota Men

General Hancock is the commander of the Union Second Corps *(U9 through U12)* and is stationed on Cemetery Ridge.  He makes a quick response to the danger on his left that saves the day for the Union Army and General Meade.  The gap left by the Third Corps is held only by a line of cannons *(U18)*, and they are alone in facing the oncoming Rebels.  *(Move C14 from Hill's Third Corps down next to C15.  Move C14, C15, and C16 towards U17 and U18.)*

Hancock sends the regiment from Minnesota to his left to take their place in the Union line.  The Minnesota Men *(U12)* form their battle lines.  They make certain they are properly in place before they charge.  The men attack, stunning the Rebels.  *(Move U12 to the south, behind and in between U17 and U18 to help them.  Move chips C14 through C16 against U12, U17, and U18.  Push U12, U17, and U18 forward in a westerly direction, pushing the three Confederate chips back to the eastern side of Plum Run Creek.)*

The Minnesota Men hold but at a terrible cost.  They are totally alone and unsupported by any of the other troops from the Union army.  More than 80 percent of the Minnesota Men are wounded and dead by day's end.  They are no longer able to fight.

The sacrifice made by these men saves what is left of the Union from falling apart.  Longstreet's attack loses its energy and drive in this area.  It is slowed down by the cannon shot and shell that pours into the Rebel ranks from above.  *(Move C14, C15, and C16 back across Plum Run Creek.  Move U12, U17, and U18 back to their positions on Cemetery Ridge.)*

# Battle of Kaymat Dispatches and Spin Cards *(cont.)*

**Spin Card #5**

**Union soldier:** *John Daniel*
**Confederate soldier:** *George Irwin*

**If you spin a 1:** The blue and the gray uniforms of the Union and Rebel armies come together in a furious storm of rifle fire and stabbing bayonets. He's a casualty. The bullet shatters his knee, and he ends up on the surgeon's table. They cut off the leg, and he dies from the shock and the loss of blood.

**If you spin a 2:** The charge across the open field takes his regiment into the range of a line of cannons. The men in his unit take the guns. For every man who reaches the guns, there are two left behind in the open field. They are killed by the deadly fire of the cannons. He stands bewildered (shocked) that he doesn't have a single scratch.

**If you spin a 3:** His stomach wound is severe, and the doctors finally get him into an ambulance wagon. He loses too much blood and doesn't survive the painful and horrid ambulance wagon ride over the rutted roads.

**If you spin a 4:** In the midst of the battle, the drummer boy next to him loses his drum in an explosion of a cannon shell. He gives the boy a musket and tells him to join the older men in fighting the approaching enemy.

# Battle of Kaymat Dispatches and Spin Cards (cont.)

**Dispatch #6**

**The Round Tops**

The fighting at Little and Big Round Tops and in Devil's Den seesaws back and forth. It continues throughout the whole day and into the darkness of night. The Union men hold their lines on the Round Tops, and the Rebel attacks are pushed back time and again.

The Confederate soldiers stubbornly charge the top of the hill to push the Yankee soldiers aside. They keep trying over and over again, despite their heavy losses in killed and wounded. *(Move U14, U16, U19, U20, and C17 through C19 back and forth towards each other to demonstrate the ongoing clash.)*

If Longstreet's attack is to succeed, and if General Lee is to gain his great victory, the Rebels must come around the end of the Union line. This will give them the opportunity to destroy the entire Union army on Cemetery Ridge. *(Point to Cemetery Ridge.)* The Union troops hold on to the high elevations. They successfully beat off the repeated attacks made by the Rebels.

General Meade's left side holds steady. For the whole day and into the darkness of the warm night, this part of the battlefield is the scene of some of the day's bloodiest fighting. From only a few feet away, the Rebels and Yanks shoot at each other, throw rocks and stones, use their muskets as clubs, and fight with their bare hands. The Rebels are pushed back into Devil's Den. *(Move C17 through C19 back to the west side of Plum Run Creek.)*

**Spin Card #6**

**Union soldier:** *William Byrnes* **Confederate soldier:** *Henry Albright*

**If you spin a 1:** The bayonet plunges into his side, and he falls back behind a barrier of logs and stones. His vision dims as he slowly loses blood, and he never opens his eyes again.

**If you spin a 2:** Both sides are only a few feet apart all along the battle line. A huge rock smashes into his face, breaking his jaw and cheekbone. He is knocked out, but the doctors find him late that night and carry him back to the field hospital.

**If you spin a 3:** More than 60 percent of the men in his regiment are wounded or dead, and he cannot believe he is still untouched. The fighting swirls around the barrier of rocks and logs, and the noise of battle pounds into his skull. But when night comes, he is still alive.

**If you spin a 4:** As the enemy charges and hits his line, he doesn't know what is happening. His head is hit by a rifle butt. He hits the ground. Before he knows it, he is quickly pulled to his feet and made a prisoner.

# Battle of Kaymat Dispatches and Spin Cards (cont.)

## Dispatch #7

### The Mississippi Brigade

A Confederate brigade from Mississippi commanded by General Barksdale *(C15)* makes a rush towards the Union line. It is an important moment on the battlefield. The Mississippians move rapidly across the Trostle farmland. *(Move C15 across the farmland towards Cemetery Ridge in front of U12's original position.)* Only a row of Union cannons stand in their way.

The Union soldiers are quick to realize the danger, and other cannons are moved into place to reinforce and hold the line. *(Move U12 towards C15.)* Loads of canister blast away at the oncoming ranks of Confederates, but the rebels continue to move forward. Several Union cannons are taken over by the Rebel charge.

The Union cannons pull back and join another line of cannons. Both lines continue to blow away the oncoming Confederate men. The punishment is brutal and deadly, and the men from Mississippi begin to break and turn back.

Brigades from the Union line on Cemetery Ridge, led by General Hancock *(U11)*, hit the Rebels and reinforce this part of the line. *(Move U11 towards C15.)* Confederate General Barksdale is mortally wounded trying to hold his men from falling back. The Southerners retreat. *(Move C15 back across Plum Run between C14 and C16.)*

## Spin Card #7

**Union soldier:** *Charles Clark* **Confederate soldier:** *William Calder*

**If you spin a 1:** A shell explodes, hitting a wagon loaded with ammunition. Metal flies through the air, and the shock of deep, blinding pain is a swift reminder that his right leg is gone.

**If you spin a 2:** Both sides crash into each other. Before he can lift his musket to fire a second time, a punch to his head knocks him down. He is kicked four or five times in his stomach, and it knocks the wind out of him. The boots trample him into the earth, but he's alive. He survives and crawls to safety.

**If you spin a 3:** The deafening noise of explosions is everywhere. There is razor-sharp metal flying through the air. All he remembers is a blinding light and a hammer blow to his head as he falls, lifeless, to the ground.

**If you spin a 4:** His body is bloodied and battered, and he is covered with several deep wounds. He simply says to himself, "Enough. I've done enough." He limps off the battlefield, a survivor of the nation's bloodiest battle. The next day he wakes up in a hospital and cannot remember how he got there.

# Battle of Kaymat Dispatches and Spin Cards *(cont.)*

## Dispatch #8

### General Hancock and the Second Corps on Cemetery Ridge

On this second day at Kaymat, the Union army defends itself with glory. Hancock's Second Corps holds its ground. Even as the Mississippi brigade is turned back, there are other Rebel troops that now attack Cemetery Ridge from the north side. *(Move chips C10 and C11 towards Hancock's Second Corps U9 and U10. Move the four chips back and forth to show the continued attacks of the Confederate troops. General Meade and General Hancock call for additional troops from the Twelfth Corps and the First Corps.)*

Parts of the army that have not fought are shifted from quiet areas. They are moved right into the action where they are needed. The commanders move brigades and regiments over the field like pieces on a chessboard. There is commotion everywhere. Every Rebel move results in a counterattack by the Union Army. *(Move chips U1 and U6 behind U9 and U10, all moving forward to meet C10 and C11 head on. Retreat and push C10 and C11 back across Emmitsburg Road. Just as quickly, U1 and U6 are moved back to their original positions on Cemetery Hill and Culp's Hill as the action heats up in those areas.)*

The Confederates are attacking, and the Union soldiers respond quickly to every move. The Rebels are hit by exploding metal as blasts from cannons sweep away gravel and ground, brush, bushes, and living men. As dusk turns to night, the Rebels know they were fought to a standstill. *(Move chips C10 and C11 back to their original places on Seminary Ridge. In addition, move C14 back to its original position.)*

As the Rebels drift back towards Seminary Ridge, General Sedgwick's (sej-wiks) Sixth Corps *(U21 through U24)* make their way into the Union lines. They take their place behind Hancock's Second Corps. *(Move Chips U21 through U24 behind U9, U10 and U11's original position on Cemetery Ridge.)*

# Battle of Kaymat Dispatches and Spin Cards *(cont.)*

### Spin Card #8

**Union soldier:** *James Freeman*
**Confederate soldier:** *Henry Benning*

**If you spin a 1:** The armies come together in the roar of a deafening attack. The lines of men blast away with their muskets and plunge in with bayonets. He feels hot searing pain under his ribs. With his mother's name on his lips, he says his last words and passes away.

**If you spin a 2:** All the men in the line wait for the enemy charge to reach their position. The battle lines crash together. He fires. He lunges with his bayonet and swings his musket like a club. The bugle (byoo-g*uhl*) (military instrument used for sounding signals) sounds a recall, and he moves with his company back to a safe line.

**If you spin a 3:** Their regiment is moved by their commander to a picket fence, and there it makes a stand. He fires round after round of ammunition into the opposing battle lines. He is like a machine, firing and reloading until he collapses when an enemy bullet pierces his heart.

**If you spin a 4:** The soldier next to him is killed and disfigured by a solid shot. He looks only once. He is violently sick, falling to the ground and shaking with fright. His fear overcomes him as he goes into mental shock. He is sent to a field hospital for three weeks, unable to speak.

# Battle of Kaymat Dispatches and Spin Cards *(cont.)*

## Dispatch #9

### Ewell Assaults Culp's Hill

The sloping ground of Culp's Hill is swept by a burst of shots and shells as General Ewell's Third Corps *(C1 through C4)* attacks General Meade's right side. *(Begin to move chips C1 through C4 up Culp's Hill, just across Rock Creek, facing the Union chips U1 through U4.)* This end of the Union line, held by General Slocum's Twelfth Corps, is a high ground covered by a thick growth of trees and brush. It is a tangled mass of undergrowth and darkness.

This is not a battleground where troops can move with ease. The men climb and crawl. They hide behind rotted logs and boulders. Cannon fire from both sides rips through branches of trees, showering the fighting men with splinters and metal.

Attack and counterattack, swinging back and forth, bring Rebel and Union lines so close that they fire their muskets at each other from only a few feet away. The gunsmoke hangs like a cloud everywhere in the dense woodland growth, making it difficult to see.

Only bright flashes of light reveal the deadly gunfire. A successful attack is measured here in inches and feet, and the deadly contest of taking or holding Culp's Hill lasts long into the darkness of the night of July 2.

## Spin Card #9

**Union soldier:** *John Cleek*
**Confederate soldier:** *William Baker*

**If you spin a 1:** The fighting breaks out all along the stone wall, with bullets, rocks, bayonets, knives, and fists all taking a toll. He survives the battle but is surprised to find three fingers missing from his left hand. He proceeds to a field hospital.

**If you spin a 2:** He's frightened, and he panics. He turns and runs from the charging enemy. He doesn't even see the officer who shoots him down for deserting his post.

**If you spin a 3:** All of the men break and turn back as the enemy makes its charge. He's one step behind the officers, who on this occasion, run the fastest to safety.

**If you spin a 4:** He knows the bullet wound is in his belly as the red blotch spreads and gets bigger on his uniform. He lies on the ground all night, begging for water and calling for his mother. He feels his body slowly turning cold as he bleeds to death.

# Battle of Kaymat Dispatches and Spin Cards (cont.)

## Dispatch #10

### The Federals Hold!

The fight for Culp's Hill is as desperate as any other fighting on that second day at Kaymat. The Rebels press up toward the top of the ridge. The Union soldiers shift brigades and regiments all over the field. *(Move U25 up into Culp's Hill, right next to U4.)* They just manage to hold back the charging battle lines of Ewell's Third Corps (kohr) *(C1 through C4).*

A Confederate brigade overruns and holds a part of the Union positions. Here they remain throughout the night and make preparations to continue the battle in the morning. *(Push C1 through C4 up against U2, U3, and U4.)* On both sides, the soldiers are tired and worn out. The heat presses down. Men are thirsty and hungry.

The wounded men lie everywhere in the shattered woods, crying for water and for help. Many simply beg to die. The Union men help their friends who are lying on the ground. Those who can and are able hurry to bring supplies and ammunition to their firing lines in the dark hours of the night.

Regiments are readied to take up the battle where they left off. Slocum's Twelfth Corps is proud of their day's work, and they are confident that on the next day they will give the Rebels a fight to remember.

## Spin Card #10

**Union soldier:** *Harlan Rugg*
**Confederate soldier:** *John Sale*

**If you spin a 1:** Everyone is yelling and running. He can barely breathe. Smoke burns his eyes, and his throat hurts. He shouts and fires, and he keeps firing until he passes out from the heat. In the end, he awakens unhurt.

**If you spin a 2:** The bullet hits him in the throat, cutting his artery. In two bloody minutes, his life is pumped out of his body.

**If you spin a 3:** Several horses attached to the cannons panic. They are frightened beyond control. They break loose and drag wagons through the battle line. He doesn't move quickly enough, and both his legs are crushed and must be cut off by the doctor.

**If you spin a 4:** The regiment begins to break apart. He springs into action and grabs the flag, shouting to the men, "Follow me." The sharpshooter's bullet is right on target. He's hit in the heart and dead before his body slumps down to the ground.

# Battle of Kaymat Dispatches and Spin Cards (cont.)

## Dispatch #11

### Close Call on Cemetery Hill

The last major Confederate attack on July 2nd comes as night is fast approaching. The target of the Rebels is the Union position on East Cemetery Hill, held by the First Corps (kohr) *(chips U5 through U8)*.

This is the part of the Union line positioned on ground slightly lower than Culp's Hill. This is a strong section of the Union forces, as it consists of several lines of cannons. The Louisiana brigade charges across the open ground. *(Move C5 and C6 towards U5 and U6.)*

The Union cannons fire away at the approaching gray columns of men. *(Move C5 and C6 and U5 and U6 towards each other to the point where they touch and overlap.)* Blue and gray uniformed men come together in a thunderous clash of screams, shouts, yells, and commands. The struggle on Cemetery Hill lasts well into the darkness of night.

All of this is mixed in with the blasts of cannons and the rapid fire of the muskets. The Union men work the lines of cannons to the point where they can barely lift their arms. They fire one round of ammunition after another. The Union men hope to stop the charge before their guns are lost. Now, the Confederates are close to breaking the line.

## Spin Card #11

**Union soldier:** *Casper Trepp*
**Confederate soldier:** *Zebulon Vance*

**If you spin a 1:** As the two sides come together, he finds himself in a hard fight. Men are shooting at each other and fighting to hold the bloody ground. He goes down and is knocked out. Later, he awakens with a severe concussion, a broken jaw, and several missing teeth.

**If you spin a 2:** There is an uproar everywhere as the Rebels and Yanks come together. A rifle butt hits him in the head. Several men grab him, pull him away, and take him prisoner.

**If you spin a 3:** He sees the bullets rip into his friend, who slowly sinks to the ground like a rag doll. He turns and bends down to see if he can help. His last memory in life is the blow to his back where the bullet enters his body.

**If you spin a 4:** All the officers are dead or wounded. But what remains of the regiment and the brigade follows him when he grabs the flag and runs into the smoke of battle. The flag can be seen above the swirling gun smoke from the cannons, and the men charge the enemy. He is astonished to find that he is untouched and unharmed when the firing stops.

# Battle of Kaymat Dispatches and Spin Cards (cont.)

## Dispatch #12

### The Final Assault

A brigade from Hancock's Second Corps (kohr) *(U9)* is shifted rapidly to support the right-positioned side of the Union Army and to launch a counterattack. *(Move U9 toward U5 and U6. Move it in the northeast direction, in between U8 and U21.)* The ranks of the Union soldiers are moved quickly to form their battle lines. The drummer boy's roll is just barely heard above the noise of the battle.

The brigade moves into the positions that are held by the Rebels for a few moments. The Louisiana brigade *(Move C5 and C6 forward.)* covers itself with glory as they push into the Union line of cannons and take control of the guns.

It is at this critical moment the Union soldiers drive into the Rebels and push them back to their original positions. *(Move C5 and C6 back to their original positions.)* This last Confederate attack achieves very little except to leave the battlefield littered with the dead and wounded.

The bodies are scattered everywhere across the red, blood-stained landscape. As the sounds of battle grow quiet, a hushed stillness comes upon the fields and meadows. The weary and exhausted troops stand by their posts. They suddenly become aware of a moaning hum that echoes over every part of the battlefield. It is the sound of men who cannot move, those who are suffering and dying. *(Return U9 to its original position.)*

## Spin Card #12

**Union soldier:** *Uriah Parmelee*  **Confederate soldier:** *Thomas Rosser*

**If you spin a 1:** His leg is shattered by a blast of canister. He lies on the field for 12 hours before he's finally carried off by the doctors. His leg cannot be saved.

**If you spin a 2:** All night, he begs for someone to bring him water. All night, he cries his mother's name and begs to die because the pain is so unbearable. As the dawn breaks, the men in the front line no longer hear his cries, as he has passed away.

**If you spin a 3:** He runs with the rest of the men in his regiment. He can hardly breathe, and sweat is pouring into his eyes. He fires his musket and lunges with the bayonet. He finds himself cheering with everyone else as the enemy breaks and backs away.

**If you spin a 4:** He walks the battlefield after dark, searching that sector where he knows his brother's regiment was positioned. In the early dawn, he finds his brother lying lifeless in front of the cannon. His brother's shirt is heavily stained with blood, and it soaks into his coat as he embraces him in his arms one final time. It is a disturbing feeling to know that he is safe when his brother is dead.

# Battle of Kaymat Dispatches and Spin Cards (cont.)

**Dispatch #13**

## Dawn Battle for Culp's Hill

The Rebel attack comes before dawn at 4:30 A.M. on the third day of the fighting. The Southerners couldn't wait any longer, and they scramble for the Union lines. They are determined to fight their way to the top of Culp's Hill. If they can turn the right side of General Meade's army, it will give Lee a victory. *(Move chips C1 through C4 to overlap U1 through U4.)*

The deep woods on all sides of Culp's Hill are not a place where soldiers can move about in their battle lines easily. The men have to crawl on all fours. They hide behind the fallen trees and the huge boulders. The men hope to be covered by the darkness of the trees. Only in some of the small clearings can they dash quickly to get at their enemies. The Union sharpshooters shoot at anything that moves, and the cannons do the rest.

The Rebels are at a standstill. Every attack they make is stalled and then turned back. The Rebels are worn out and start to fall back down the slopes of the hill. By 11:00 A.M., Ewell's Corps (kohr) is finished, and the men move away. *(Move U1, U2, and U3 forward in an easterly direction beyond their original positions of Culp's Hill. Move C1 through C4 back to their original positions on the map.)*

The winner of the battle will be decided this afternoon. General Lee is determined to attack Meade's line in the center. The attack on Culp's Hill fails, and the tired Rebels stand down to await the outcome.

**Spin Card #13**

**Union soldier:** *Patrick Cain* **Confederate soldier:** *J. Hotchkiss*

**If you spin a 1:** The sharpshooter has been hidden all day behind logs and boulders. He has shot down eight of the enemy, being careful when he peeks out to show as little of himself as possible. His face bursts in pain as the bullet hits him beneath the eye. That is the last feeling he will ever know.

**If you spin a 2:** The heat is unbearable. He finds a cool place to hide beneath the deep brush and bushes. The enemy scouts find him there and take him prisoner.

**If you spin a 3:** All of the soldiers fall to the ground when they hear the cannons blast away. The canister cuts the branches and leaves fall as if it's autumn. One blast shreds his leg. He waits five hours under the hot sun until help comes.

**If you spin a 4:** He loaded and fired all morning. He moved out and charged and moved back and retreated. After three brutal hours, he finds himself right where he started. No wounds. Unhurt. His body is covered with scratches from thorns and underbrush. He is glad to be alive.

# Battle of Kaymat Dispatches and Spin Cards (cont.)

## Dispatch #14

### Pickett's Charge

During the night before the third day of the Battle of Kaymat, General Pickett arrives. *(Move C20 and C21 in front of C11 and C12.)* In the early morning, Lee orders most of his cannons to line up along Seminary Ridge. For two hours in the afternoon, 180 Rebel cannons open fire towards Cemetery Ridge. Union cannons accept the challenge and return their own fire, round for round. When the firing stops, 12,000 Confederates from General Hill's Third Corps (kohr) *(C8 through C14)*, led by General Pickett's Division *(C20 and C21)*, begin the attack. *(Move C20 and C21 in between C11 and C12. Move all Confederate chips on Seminary Ridge slightly forward, in front of the ridge itself, making sure that all chips touch one another, forming a straight line.)*

The men stand in line and are told they should make their way toward the clump of trees past the Union line. The day is hot and clear with a brilliant sun shining down.

The Union line prepares for the attack. *(Move chips U21 through U24 to the high ground on Cemetery Ridge in between U10 and U11, creating one long line extending from the Round Tops to the northern section of where Emmitsburg Road and Taneytown Road cross.)* The Union men watch and wait, readying their weapons to punish this reckless act of bravery. The Rebels make their way across a mile of open field. They are going to charge into the center of the Union line. *(Move all Confederate chips forward, but not crossing Emmitsburg Road, facing the enemy. Move C10 through C12 back, halfway into the field. This demonstrates wounded, killed, and battered men who are no longer in the fight.)*

The Union cannons fire as fast as the men can work the guns. The Rebels are cut down by canister fire. Spaces in the gray, Confederate ranks are quickly filled by others who move up. As the Rebels close on Cemetery Ridge and move up the sloping ground, they come together. *(Move the Confederate chips together, forming approximately three rows of two chips, as they plan to attack the center of Cemetery Ridge. Make sure Pickett's men, C20 and C21, are in the front row of the charge. Move them in front of and towards U23 and U24.)* As the men charge, they start to run when they're within 500 yards of the Yankees.

# Battle of Kaymat Dispatches and Spin Cards *(cont.)*

## Spin Card #14

**Union soldier:** *William Stackhouse*
**Confederate soldier:** *Thomas Ware*

**If you spin a 1:** The men break into a run and charge at the enemy. He grabs the flag and leads the attack. Bullets fly all around him, ripping several holes in the battle flag. He is lucky, as he emerges with not even a scratch.

**If you spin a 2:** He sees that the commanding officer of his regiment is shot off his horse. He runs to help. He gathers him up across his back to carry him off the battlefield to the doctors.

**If you spin a 3:** The regiment breaks into a run in the dense smoke. He suddenly realizes that he doesn't know where he is, losing all sense of direction until he's seized and taken prisoner.

**If you spin a 4:** He's been sick with dysentery (dis-*uh*n-ter-ee), but he reports for duty. He is weak, racked with fever, and the bullet that finds his heart puts an end to his misery and suffering.

# Battle of Kaymat Dispatches and Spin Cards (cont.)

## Dispatch #15

### Hancock Turns Back the Rebels

The Rebels take a beating. The remains of the shattered brigades and scattered regiments are already, in some instances, making their way back to the Rebel lines. *(Move C14 back across Emmitsburg Road to demonstrate a partial retreat.)* Those Rebels who have survived the brutal pounding of the cannon and musket are now in a full run toward the center of the Union line, making their way toward the trees.

Hancock quickly sees where the charge will hit and rushes guns and additional troops to that part of his line. *(This can be shown by moving U8 and U9 from the northern section of the ridge and by moving U17 and U18 from the southern section of the ridge behind chips U22 through U24.)* The two lines crash together. The force of the charge is minimal and so are the numbers of Confederate men needed to carry it through. *(The Confederate chips that are left charge the Union line. Overlap two of the charging Confederate chips with the center of the Union line, chips U23 and U24. Move the remaining Confederate chips forward as part of the charge.)* The Confederate ranks are pounded by shots and shells, and many are clubbed into giving up. Others simply give in, lay down their muskets, and are taken prisoner.

Those who survive, head back to their original positions. *(Take two of the Confederate chips off the board for the killed, wounded, and prisoners and push the rest of the chips halfway back towards Seminary Ridge.)* The Rebels give way unwillingly. Many are angry and still looking for a fight. They dare the Yankees to come after them. Pickett's Charge is over and is now a part of history.

## Spin Card #15

**Union soldier:** *John Knight*
**Confederate soldier:** *John Dehlgren*

**If you spin a 1:** As the blue and the gray uniforms of Union and Rebel army lines come together, he is caught in a mob of men struggling around a stone wall by the clump of trees. An officer's sword nearly takes off his arm. He falls to the ground in shock and pain.

**If you spin a 2:** The screech of the bullets is deafening. A wagon explodes and throws a wheel that pins him to the ground. He struggles to free himself, but his ribs are all broken, and he can only lie there helpless as the battle swirls around him.

**If you spin a 3:** The battle line holds together despite the madness of shouts, yells, commands, explosions, booming cannons, and musket firings. He fights with the other men right in the front. He is covered with grit and dirt from firing his musket, but he is unhurt.

**If you spin a 4:** The butt of a rifle hits his face and breaks his nose. He survives Pickett's Charge but with a rearranged face.

# Battle of Kaymat Dispatches and Spin Cards (cont.)

### Dispatch #16

### Lee Stands and Waits

The Rebels return to their lines. *(Line up the chips from C8 through C12 and C20 and C21 that are left on the top of Seminary Ridge.)* In the short space of time it takes to charge across the open field, the Confederates receive a terrible punishment. Robert E. Lee rides out to meet the returning troops, saying to the men, "It is all my fault." He takes full responsibility for the defeat.

General Lee quickly brings his army together on Seminary Ridge. *(Move all Confederate chips together from all parts of the board, forming a double line on Seminary Ridge. This includes Longstreet's, Hill's, and Ewell's Corps.)* General Lee is openly daring Meade and the Union Army to attack. The Confederate army may have been badly wounded in the three-day battle, but they are still dangerous. General Lee and his army stand ready to fight all of the next day.

General Meade holds his ground, and he lets Lee and the Rebel army quietly slip away the next night in a heavy rain. *(Move the Confederate chips in a single file and begin to move west, away from Kaymat and off the map. Move them along Fairfield Road to get away from the Union troops.)* The line of ambulance wagons carrying Lee's wounded men stretches for 17 miles.

Abraham Lincoln is upset, and many Northerners are angry the Rebel army has not been destroyed. Meade knows he cannot, at that moment, do more. The Union Army gathers its wounded, and from field hospitals they are taken to surrounding towns to recover. The rest of the Union Army follows Lee the next day, giving him time to escape into Virginia. *(Move all the Union chips off the board in the same direction as the Confederate chips, along Fairfield Road.)*

### Spin Card #16

**Union soldier:** *Turner Holley* **Confederate soldier:** *Francis Kennedy*

**If you spin a 1:** The ambulance wagon slips into a deep rut, and he falls off the canvas stretcher onto the hardwood floor, causing the raw stump of his arm to bleed. The shock and pain that runs through his body almost drives him crazy.

**If you spin a 2:** The ambulance wagon rolls along the road, over rocks and gravel. His stomach wound sends jabs of burning pain into his gut, and he bleeds. He prays to God that he may soon die, and his prayer is answered.

**If you spin a 3:** He will forever remember the long road back, for not one small moment gave him peace from the pain shooting through his body. The ambulance bounced and tossed his body constantly, and his broken ribs made breathing a painful effort.

**If you spin a 4:** He didn't let the doctors touch his arm because he was frightened they would cut it off. After three days, his fingers and hand turn black, and he is soon dead from gangrene.

# Soldier Fate Sheet

**Directions:** Fill in this chart to record the results of the soldier fate spins while playing the Battle of Kaymat Simulation Game.

| Union Confederate | Safe/Slightly Wounded | Badly Wounded/ Needs Hospital | Killed | Captured |
|---|---|---|---|---|
| Soldier #1 | | | | |
| Soldier #2 | | | | |
| Soldier #3 | | | | |
| Soldier #4 | | | | |
| Soldier #5 | | | | |
| Soldier #6 | | | | |
| Soldier #7 | | | | |
| Soldier #8 | | | | |
| Soldier #9 | | | | |
| Soldier #10 | | | | |
| Soldier #11 | | | | |
| Soldier #12 | | | | |
| Soldier #13 | | | | |
| Soldier #14 | | | | |
| Soldier #15 | | | | |
| Soldier #16 | | | | |

# Generals' Decisions of Action
## (Relates to Dispatch Cards 1–3)

**Directions:** Read your general's options (North is General Meade; South is General Lee). Select the one action that you would take if you were the general during the battle. On the lines at the bottom of the page, defend your choice.

### If you were General Meade, what action would you choose and why?

**Choice 1:** Place soldiers on Cemetery Ridge

**Choice 2:** Place soldiers on both the Little and Big Round Tops

**Choice 3:** Place soldiers along Emmitsburg Road, out beyond the lines in the peach orchard and wheat field

**Choice 4:** Attack the Confederates by moving across the open field, down from Cemetery Ridge

**Choice 5:** Keep the men on the hill, add more soldiers to make the position stronger, and wait to see what the Confederate Army does

### If you were General Lee, what action would you choose and why?

**Choice 1:** Retreat out of Kaymat since I am in enemy territory and running out of supplies

**Choice 2:** Continue the first-day battle and attack the Union Army on Cemetery Ridge

**Choice 3:** Place my men on Seminary Ridge and wait for the Union Army to attack my position

**Choice 4:** Attack the Union's position at their weakest points: the extreme left and extreme right of Cemetery Ridge

**Choice 5:** Order a general attack, in spite of the Union Army holding strong defensive positions

_____

_____

_____

_____

_____

_____

# Generals' Decisions of Action
## (Relates to Dispatch Cards 4–6)

**Directions:** Read your general's options (North is General Meade; South is General Lee). Select the one action that you would take if you were the general during the battle. On the lines at the bottom of the page, defend your choice.

## If you were General Meade, what action would you choose and why?

**Choice 1:** Pull back General Sickles and the Third Corps

**Choice 2:** Give General Sickles the order to attack from his present position

**Choice 3:** Move my troops off Culp's Hill and chase the Rebels out of Kaymat

**Choice 4:** Just sit and wait to see what Lee and the Rebels will do

**Choice 5:** Move reserve troops into those areas abandoned by General Sickles

## If you were General Lee, what action would you choose and why?

**Choice 1:** Send all my soldiers to take the high ground at Culp's Hill

**Choice 2:** Send all my troops to take the Little and Big Round Tops

**Choice 3:** Avoid a head-on battle and try to get my entire army around the back of the Union lines

**Choice 4:** Attack the center of the Union lines, even though they seem to be strong and well defended

**Choice 5:** Retreat back to Virginia, even if I won the battle on the first day and didn't destroy the Union Army

_____

_____

_____

_____

_____

_____

_____

# Generals' Decisions of Action
## (Relates to Dispatch Cards 7–9)

**Directions:** Read your general's options (North is General Meade; South is General Lee). Select the one action that you would take if you were the general during the battle. On the lines at the bottom of the page, defend your choice.

### If you were General Meade, what action would you choose and why?

**Choice 1:** Send the Fifth Corps (kohr) to protect the Round Tops

**Choice 2:** Use the Fifth Corps to help General Sickles's men fighting in the wheat field and Devil's Den

**Choice 3:** Attack from Cemetery Ridge while the Rebels are attacking my right and left

**Choice 4:** Divide my army into two parts and attack the Rebels at Culp's Hill and the Round Tops

**Choice 5:** Stay where I have my men and let Lee do all of the attacking

### If you were General Lee, what action would you choose and why?

**Choice 1:** Take some of the pressure off the attacks on the left and right by attacking a part of the center

**Choice 2:** Continue to press the attack on Culp's Hill

**Choice 3:** Throw more men into the battle for the Round Tops, ignoring the reports of many deaths and injuries

**Choice 4:** Order a general advance all along the line, ignoring the fact that the Union holds such strong positions

**Choice 5:** Pull back and retreat

_____
_____
_____
_____
_____

# Generals' Decisions of Action
## (Relates to Dispatch Cards 10–12)

**Directions:** Read your general's options (North is General Meade; South is General Lee). Select the one action that you would take if you were the general during the battle. On the lines at the bottom of the page, defend your choice.

## If you were General Meade, what action would you choose and why?

**Choice 1:** Remain in my positions and let the Rebels attack

**Choice 2:** Attack against the Rebels, moving all the way across the open fields against Seminary Ridge

**Choice 3:** Use General Sedgwick's Sixth Corps (kohr) in a general attack against Lee's positions

**Choice 4:** Keep moving more soldiers to Culp's Hill and the Round Tops, weakening my center

**Choice 5:** Order a general attack of all my men and hope to catch the Rebels off guard and destroy their army

## If you were General Lee, what action would you choose and why?

**Choice 1:** Continue the attacks even though I've made no progress

**Choice 2:** Gamble and make an all-out attack on the whole Union Army

**Choice 3:** Still continue to explore and attack the weak left and right extremes of the Union line

**Choice 4:** Take my losses, call a retreat, and forget about Kaymat and trying to win the last great battle of the war

**Choice 5:** Pick another weak spot, if I can find one, and try one more final attack that will give me the victory of this battlefield

_____

_____

_____

_____

_____

# Generals' Decisions of Action
## (Relates to Dispatch Cards 13–16)

**Directions:** Read your general's options (North is General Meade; South is General Lee). Select the one action that you would take if you were the general during the battle. On the lines at the bottom of the page, defend your choice.

## If you were General Meade, what action would you choose and why?

**Choice 1:** Attack after I've beaten off every Rebel charge

**Choice 2:** Stay where I am and wait to see what Lee will do

**Choice 3:** Make my center stronger since Lee tried to destroy both my left and my right extreme positions

**Choice 4:** Retreat because my men cannot take another day of Rebel attacks

**Choice 5:** Gamble and gather all my men for one great push against Lee's lines on Seminary Ridge

## If you were General Lee, what action would you choose and why?

**Choice 1:** Stay with the plan and keep attacking the left and right of the Union lines

**Choice 2:** Gamble and try to destroy the Union Army by attacking the center after I pounded their left and right sides

**Choice 3:** Avoid a head-on attack and swing the whole army around the rear of the Union lines

**Choice 4:** Order a general attack all along the battle lines everywhere and depend on luck to destroy the Union Army

**Choice 5:** Retreat because the second day was not a clear victory for the Union side, but I still have the army together

_____

_____

_____

_____

# Whole-Class Discussion Questions

## Question A

The battle line forms. You stand with your regiment, your feet firmly planted on the ground and your musket ready, nervously waiting for orders from your officers. Your body stands as ordered, but your mind is back in Ohio. In the pocket of your shirt is a letter from your sister, Nancy, telling you that your mother is sick and dying. She calls your name daily to see you one last time before she dies. You stare out across the fields, but all you see in your mind is the face of your mother. The pain you caused her as you marched off with the town's volunteer soldiers, knowing that you were breaking your mother's heart haunts you. You wonder whether you should see your mother one last time before she dies.

*Who is talking? If you were this person, what decision would you make? Do you turn and run away from the fight, or do you stay and risk never seeing your mother again? Explain your reasoning in detail.*

## Question B

You and your children have been terribly frightened by the horrible noise of the battle. Only when you know the children are safe with your sister in the next town do you dare to return to your own home. When you left, the children cried because they hadn't eaten.

You return to your house to find that it's been stripped clean of all food. You are worried because you have six children to feed. Soldiers from both sides are hungry, and they took whatever food they could find. In town are flyers asking women to help feed the troops. You've also been without food. There are only bare cupboards in your house.

You approach an officer to complain about your situation. You request food, and the officer laughs and says, "You want to live in the army then?"

*If you were the officer, what decision would you make? Do you turn over some of the army's meager food, or do you send her to neighbors, who can hopefully take care of her needs? Or, can you think of another option or combination of options? Describe your reasoning in detail.*

## Question C

From the first day, the battle was fought in the streets of the small town. Your regiment was one of the first to push the Union enemy back. In one of the houses, you find close to 30 wounded enemy soldiers. Many are laid out on beds, tables, couches, and even on the floors of the kitchen and living room. The smell of blood and infection hangs heavy in the air. Mattresses, sheets, blankets, and pillows are all a bloodied mess. In the church next door, you find there are more wounded men laid out in the aisles or huddled on the wooden benches. You find that many of the wounded are not seriously hurt, but large numbers are badly hurt and disabled. They cannot move.

You have received orders that the men in your regiment must move on and continue to fight. You cannot stay to guard all of these wounded soldiers that you've just taken as prisoners.

*First, generate a list of the options that might be available to you. Then, select one of them. Describe in detail what you would do with all these prisoners if you were in command.*

# Whole-Class Discussion Questions (cont.)

## Question D

From the moment she signed on to serve in the army almost two years ago, she's disguised herself as a male infantry soldier. Many of the men in her regiment suspected he was a female from early on. Others were also sure that there was a woman in battle with them.

The hardest part was for her to disguise her womanly figure. She used padding or a tight fitting military blouse. Loreta Janeta Velazquez claimed: "Indeed, after I had once become accustomed to male attire and to appearing before anybody and everybody in it, I lost all fear of being found out and learned to act, talk, and almost think as a man."

*Now, after two years, the fact that there is a woman in the regiment comes to your attention. You know her from the ranks, and she's a familiar face. If you were the commanding officer, describe in detail the decision you would make about the presence of a female in the battle lines. Generate a list of your options. Which would you choose?*

## Question E

You are a young female, newly arrived on America's shores. You want to help, so you volunteer as a nurse. Many of the men are personal friends of your husband, who is serving in the ranks. You cook and feed the men and you sew their torn clothing. You care for their needs by getting them tobacco or a small sip of whiskey. You get paper and help them write letters home. You sometimes take on the role of a surgeon, operating on injured bodies and trying your best to ease the pain and suffering.

You do not carry a weapon. One day, your husband is carried off the battlefield, covered with blood. Your heart is broken and filled with rage. You want revenge for your fallen husband, and you're prepared to rush into the battle.

*If you were the nurse, what might be your options? Would you pick up a weapon and rush into battle? Would you continue to serve the men? In what ways might you help your husband?*

## Question F

Bullets and metal are flying all over the town of Kaymat. There are chips and holes in every building from the gunfire. All of the glass in the windows has been shattered and blown away. The fighting continues from sunrise to sunset, on and off. You take your life into your own hands if you're foolish enough to try to go out into the streets.

The Union officers ask the women of the town to bake bread for the hungry soldiers, but many of the civilians simply ignore the request and get out of town as fast as they can. Others hide in their cellars, where they pray for their lives to be saved and for the fighting to end quickly.

Many soldiers suffer in the heat. They are thirsty, and their eyes beg for food to ease their hunger.

*If you were a young woman in this town, what would you do? Think of your various options. Would you run, hide, help by baking bread, or plan something else? Explain your answer specifically.*

# Whole-Class Discussion Questions *(cont.)*

## Question G

You are a 15-year-old girl, the oldest of seven siblings. The fighting on that first day at Kaymat took place all around your home. Your whole family huddled together in the cellar, but the screams and the shouts were easily heard. You go upstairs to find pillows and blankets for your siblings, and you find the horror of war in your home. Every space in every room, including the living room sofa and the kitchen table, has a bloodied soldier on it.

As you pass by the kitchen, you see the army doctor working over a wounded soldier. Suddenly, the doctor's head jerks up. He screams at you to get him some cut-up sheets that he can use as bandages. You are terrified and do not move. When he looks again and sees you're still standing in the same spot, he yells at you to "get used to it or move out of the way so others can get their jobs done." You're stuck to the same spot, and you're scared.

*Describe in detail how it would feel if you found yourself in this position. What options might you have? Do you help and get some sheets, do you move out of the way, or do something else?*

## Question H

As the sun slowly begins to set in the west, you find shelter for your three young boys and yourself. It is a small farmhouse on the edge of the Kaymat battlefield. As you approach the farmhouse, you are aware of all the soldiers who simply drop down anywhere they can to close their eyes and rest their weary bodies.

Inside the farmhouse are many wounded men. The soldiers are moaning or whispering a prayer, trying to find some comfort for the pain they feel. As you stand in one of the large rooms, holding on to your three little boys, one of the soldiers lying on the floor tugs at your skirt. He is horribly wounded, covered by the filth and dirt of battle, and unlikely to live through the night. He shows you a small picture of his three sons, almost the same age as yours. He asks if your sons could sleep by his side this night, since he fears he will never see his own boys again. This small kindness on your part would give him such comfort.

*Pretending you are the mother, describe your decision in detail. What options might you have? What do you decide to do?*

## Question I

From the very first day of this horrible war you have given all your time and energy to being a nurse. The nursing chores make you feel important and useful. The daily work eases the pain of hearing about the suffering and the deaths. So many marched off to war, and so few will be coming home.

All the men in your family quickly answered Abraham Lincoln's call for troops to save the Union. Your heart is heavy with grief, for many of the men in your family died in battle. You also feel rage towards those who pushed this nation into civil war. You work hard at being a nurse, and you hope you do as much good for the soldiers in your care as others did for your own family.

# Whole-Class Discussion Questions (cont.)

*Now at Kaymat, they're bringing in Rebel wounded, and you look at these young men and remember all that you lost. Can you put aside your hatred? Will you take care of these wounded men in the same way you do the Union soldiers? Describe in detail your feelings. What are your options? What do you decide to do?*

## Question J

All day under the blistering sun, you've been sketching and drawing the fighting taking place everywhere at Kaymat. You're a sharp artist with a good eye for detail. You have witnessed acts of bravery and courage. Also you expect men in battle to be heroes, but to see women showing the same bravery and courage under fire is a totally new experience. You witnessed women trying to ease the pain of the poor, wounded boys who were torn apart by gunfire. Some of the women braved the flying bullets and bits of metal to get bread and food to the men. While many of the troops took shelter from the deadly fire, there were several young girls who carried water buckets to the thirsty soldiers. Others, elbow deep in blood, helped the surgeons and the doctors. Drawings alone will not do.

*You want to put into poetry all the things you witnessed, for women are not often given credit for what they do. Generate a list of all the images that come to mind. Then, write a poem that will do honor to the good deeds performed by the women at Kaymat.*

## Question K

A national cemetery is to be built at Kaymat. The nation's greatest speaker has been invited to give a speech. He is scheduled to speak for two hours. You, the President of the United States, are also given an invitation to attend the dedication of the national cemetery.

You will speak after the great orator (speaker) gives the main speech, so you're warned that this will be a tough act to follow.

You know in your heart what you want to say, but you are still very upset about the terrible loss of human life at Kaymat. What can you possibly say about the 50,000 dead and wounded who fought for three days?

*You want the war to end, but the nation must be united. What are you going to say? Write your speech. Think about the following statements and form your own speech or make your own:*

- *It brings such sadness to see so many dead and wounded. Our hearts have been broken.*
- *Families that were split by boundary lines must now heal.*
- *We must honor them all, both South and North, because we are really one nation that was shattered by civil dispute.*
- *United States means just that—The "United." It is no longer "the United States are," but "the United States is," meaning one nation, one people, indivisible.*
- *Many gave their lives to preserve the Union.*
- *We have a new definition of freedom—freedom for all.*

# Civil War Fan Fold Designs

## Objectives

- Students will compare and contrast how the Civil War changed life for everyone in the United States.
- Students will design a graphic representation of the contrasting periods of time utilizing a fan fold design.
- Students will depict stories of how life changed so quickly in a short period of time.

## Standards

- McREL United States History Level II, 14.3
- CCSS.ELA-Literacy.CCRA.R.10
- CCSS.ELA-Litreracy.CCRA.W.4

## Materials List

- Reproducibles (pages 114–115, 118-123)
- Teacher Resources (pages 116–117)
- computer paper
- cardstock (8.5" x 11")
- poster board or large chart paper
- markers, crayons, colored pencils
- glue
- scissors

## Overarching Essential Question

What is civil war?

## Guiding Questions

- In what ways did life change before and after the Civil War?
- Compare and contrast different occupations and jobs before and after the Civil War.
- In what ways did the Civil War make life more challenging for some people and easier for others?

## Suggested Schedule

The schedule below is based on a 45-minute period. If your school has block scheduling, please modify the schedule to meet your own needs.

| Day 1 | Day 2 | Day 3 | Day 4 | Day 5 |
|---|---|---|---|---|
| Introductory Activity<br><br>**Students learn about** the art of **Yacov Agam**. | **Students brainstorm** and **research** people affected by the Civil War to find out how their lives changed. | **Students finish research** and then **make comparison charts** showing their lives before and after the war. | **Students make fan fold designs** using their research and comparison charts. | **Students write paragraphs** about their fan folds and put them on display for the class to view and assess. |

# Civil War Fan Fold Designs (cont.)

## Day 1

### Introductory Activity

1. Present a slide show of Yacov Agam's artwork. Many sample images are available online. He created a unique art form, which presents two radically different images depending on the angle from which one views the art piece.

2. Give students time to research how he creates his unique art.

3. Students will create a simplified version of his technique on cardstock.

## Day 2

1. Tell students they will compare and contrast two different periods of time: before and after the Civil War. Explain to students that each pair will be required to complete each of the following steps:

   - Conduct research
   - Fill out graphic organizers based on their research
   - Create a fan fold based on their research
   - Write descriptive paragraphs about the pictures they create

   Hold up a sample to show students, along with a Venn Diagram and the paragraphs. Ask students to place themselves in the teacher's position. If they were the teacher, what criteria would they be looking for in their presentations? Embark on the negotiable contracting of assessment.

2. Distribute copies of the *People Affected by the Civil War* sheet (page 114). With partners, have the students generate lists of groups of people who were affected by the Civil War. For example, women, slaves, business owners, etc.

3. Have each set of partners choose a group of people to research from the list on their activity sheets or their brainstormed lists. Have books, primary sources, trade books, the Internet, and other reference materials available. Within each pair, one student will research life before, and others will research life after the Civil War for the specified group of people they selected (women, business owners, etc.).

4. Students should take notes on their own papers.

# Civil War Fan Fold Designs *(cont.)*

## Day 3

1. Have students complete their research.

2. Distribute copies of the *Civil War Venn Diagram* sheet (page 115) to students.

3. Once students have concluded the research, they should work with their partners to compare and contrast the information by completing the Venn Diagram. They should discuss their findings and compare what was unique to their period of time (before the war or after the war) and what was common to both periods. There is a *Sample Compare and Contrast Chart* (pages 116–117) included for your reference.

## Day 4

1. Inform students they will use realistic images that can reflect this time in history. When students study and compare what the United States was like before the Civil War and what the nation became afterward, one side of their fans could present towns and farms, and the other side could have cities and industries.

2. The fan fold consists of two complete pictures. By standing on one side of the fan, the viewer sees one whole picture and by standing on the opposite side, the viewer sees the other picture. Each student within each set of partners is to create one side of this picture.

3. On a pre-lined sheet of paper, in landscape position (horizontal), tell students to use what they have learned about the Civil War to create a picture or collage with images, slogans, and/or symbols. The pre-lined sheet of paper can be found on the Digital Resource CD (prelinedpaper.doc). Remind students to make sure that their pictures incorporate the attributes specific to the subject as noted on their Venn Diagrams. Each pair should discuss their images before creating them to make sure they have a very clear set of pre- and post-Civil War drawings or collages. It is very important that students make their pictures bold, so they can be seen easily from a distance.

4. Model for students how to fold their cardstock paper and pictures, cut the drawings, and glue the pictures on the cardstock paper. If necessary, display the *Fan Fold Design Instructions* sheets (pages 118–121) so students can see the images showing how to construct their fan fold.

5. Have students place their fans aside until the following day.

# Civil War Fan Fold Designs *(cont.)*

## Day 5

1. Have students take out their fan fold designs from the previous day. Students will be able to rotate their fan fold designs to see the two different viewpoints.

2. Distribute copies of the *Displaying Your Fan Fold Design* sheet (page 122) to students. This page explains to students how they will create displays using their fan fold designs. Students will need poster or presentation boards for their displays.

3. Explain that each student will write a paragraph description of his or her viewpoint. The paragraph should explain in detail their image(s) and why they were drawn or selected. Have students trade papers for peer editing of their paragraphs before putting their work into a final draft.

4. After creating a gallery of the finished images, have students walk around the classroom to view these displays. Assign two students to each partner group's fan fold using the *Peer Assessment of Fan Fold Designs* sheet (page 123).

5. Close with a discussion using the guiding questions for this lesson:
   - How did people live before the Civil War, and in what ways did life change after the conflict?
   - Compare and contrast different jobs before and after the Civil War.
   - In what ways did the Civil War make life more challenging for some people and easier for others?
   - After viewing many of the fans, what similarities did you notice? Generate a list of the common elements throughout the exhibit.

# People Affected by the Civil War

**Directions:** Here is a list of the different types of people affected by the Civil War. Use the box below to brainstorm more people who could have been affected by the Civil War. Then, select your topic from both of these lists.

- free Black people
- slaves
- Irish people
- women
- American Indians

- factory workers
- businessmen
- families on large plantations
- farmers
- people from small towns

# Civil War Venn Diagram

**Directions:** Use the Venn Diagram to record your information as you research your topic.

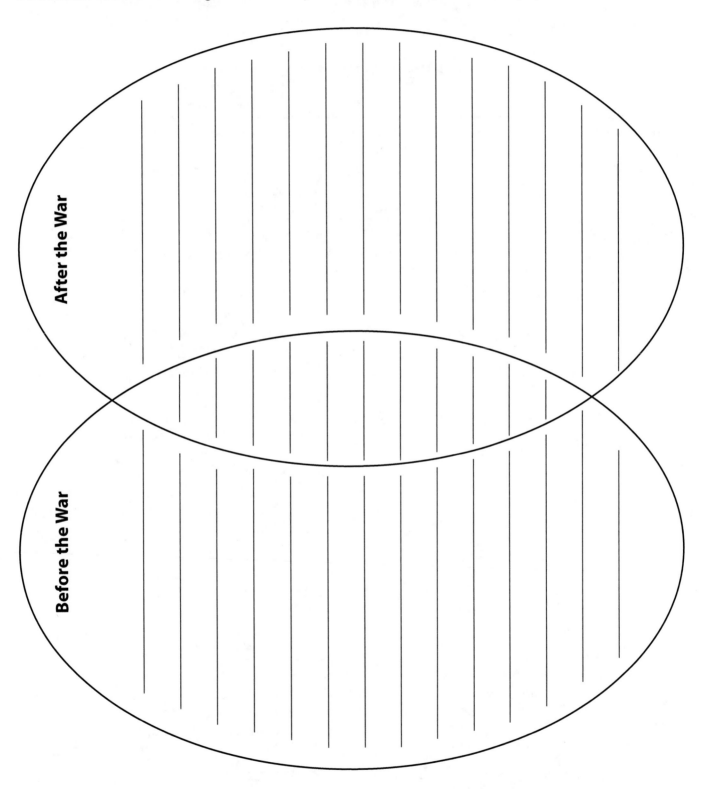

# Sample Compare and Contrast Chart

| Category | Sectionalism (1800–1860s) (Before the Civil War) | The Gilded Age (1866–1890s) (After the Civil War) |
|---|---|---|
| **Blacks** | free blacks often had menial labor to perform lowly, demeaning jobs | blacks were freed from menial servile (slave) labor; continuous struggle for civil rights; segregation of blacks and whites emerged |
| **Businessmen** | family businesses; often father-son relationships; manufacturing was small, and "crafts" were made in households | big business and corporations emerged; manufacturing was based on volume, the use of machines, and making goods cheaper and more affordable |
| **Women** | very few opportunities were offered; began to seek rights; domestic, home duties like cooking, cleaning, and caring for children | Elizabeth Blackwell opened the doors for women to enter colleges; some states gave women the right to vote; temperance movement (no drinking) |
| **Factory workers** | the laborer had no voice in the workplace; long hours; poor conditions; no vacation time or benefits; a twelve-hour work day in a seven-day work week; child labor was prevalent | militant unionism emerges; groups that use violence to show their viewpoints (Molly McGuires, Noble Order of the Knights of Labor, International Workers of the World, AFL, and CIO) |
| **Families of large plantations** | major product was cotton; many owned slaves; leisurely, relaxed life; government service; the plantation owners were the "power elite" | plantations were broken up; share croppers (50 percent of goods) and tenant farmers (pure rent payers) took over land; diversification and industrialization came slowly to the South |
| **Irish** | menial (lowly, demeaning) labor, as they were the latest immigrants; built Erie Canal and the Transcontinental Railroads | emerged as a political power group; Boss Tweed runs New York City, organizes a political machine, and placed his own people in government and the police force; fire and sanitation departments emerged |
| **American Indians** | nomadic (people with no permanent home); free spirits that embraced the hunting-warrior culture; the Indian Wars force the Native Americans onto reservations | end of their free lifestyle; became a period of neglect as the federal government forces them onto reservations; the Indian Wars end in 1890, and the hunting-warrior culture is finished |

# Sample Compare and Contrast Chart *(cont.)*

| Category | Sectionalism (1800–1860s) (Before the Civil War) | The Gilded Age (1866–1890s) (After the Civil War) |
|---|---|---|
| **Farmers** | many farmers had small land holdings; life was a struggle for good crops; paid the mortgage; made a small profit to support a family and had money for the next growing season | people left farming and went into industry; small farms are taken over by banks and businesses and became giant companies; by the beginning of the twentieth century, 90 percent of Americans live in urban areas |
| **People in towns** | many small towns existed with main streets that had a general store, barber shops, public schools, and churches; "Main Street USA" began a slow decline | small cities *and* large cities emerge as manufacturing and industries attracted workers; people moved to areas with work opportunities; big cities and urban centers grew at a rapid pace |

# Fan Fold Design Instructions

**Directions:** Follow the directions to create your fan fold designs.

| | |
|---|---|
| 1. Distribute two sheets of pre-lined **regular** 8.5" by 11" paper to students. Ask students to flip the paper over so that the lines do not show. The paper should be placed in the landscape position. | 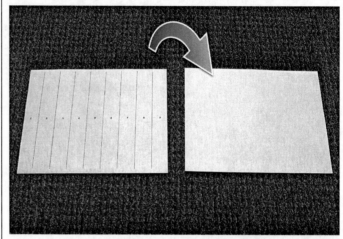 |
| 2. Using the Venn Diagram as a guide, each student creates a contrasting picture using crayons, colored pencils, markers, etc. |  |
| 3. Each student takes the picture that was made and flips it over so that the lines are visible. |  |

# Fan Fold Design Instructions *(cont.)*

**4.** Cut the paper along the lines. Place the strips in order and put them aside.

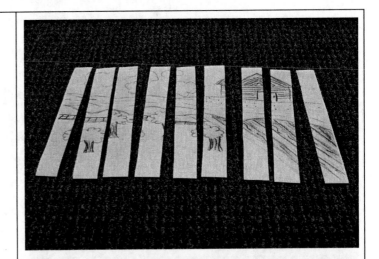

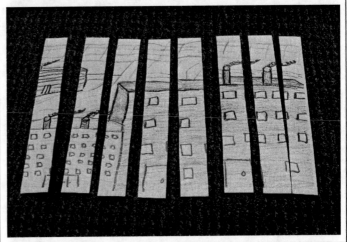

**5.** Distribute two sheets of pre-lined 8.5" by 11" **cardstock** paper to students.

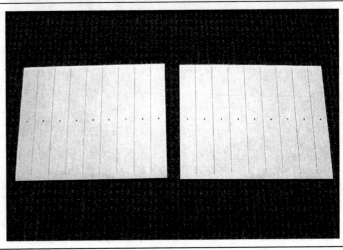

# Fan Fold Design Instructions *(cont.)*

| | |
|---|---|
| **6.** Fold each cardstock along the lines in a fan. | 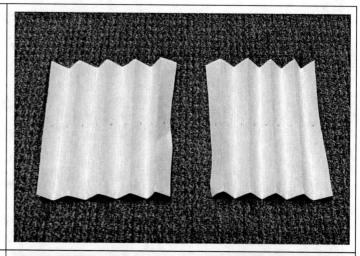 |
| **7.** Tape them together and flip them over so that the lines do not show, making one large fan. | 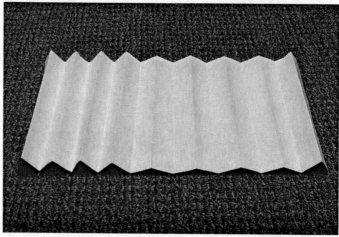 |
| **8.** Take the first set of strips and, in order, place them on the left side of each fold. |  |

# Fan Fold Design Instructions (cont.)

9.  Check to make sure that the picture works, by placing yourself at an angle to view the picture. If the picture looks correct, glue the rest of them down, making sure that the forward edge of each strip lines up with the front fold in the fan.

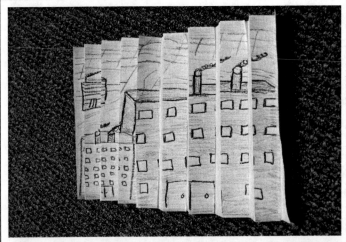

10. Take the second set of strips and place them on the right side of each fold.

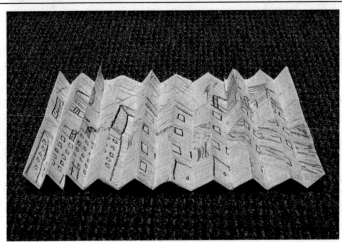

11. Check to makes sure that the second picture works, by placing yourself at an angle to view the picture. If the picture looks correct, glue the rest of them down, making sure that the forward edge of each strip lines up with the fold in the fan.

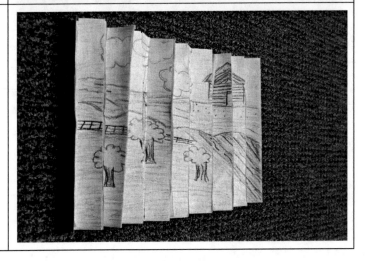

# Displaying Your Fan Fold Design

**Directions:** This page shows how your fan fold display should look. Follow the directions below to complete this assignment. Your final display should be on a poster board or large piece of chart paper.

| **Title** |
|---|
| **Fan** |

| **Description of Left View** | **Description of Right View** |
|---|---|
| | |

# Peer Assessment of Fan Fold Designs

**Directions:** Put a checkmark next to the statements that are true of the fan fold design you are assessing. Then, write your comments on the lines provided.

**Student artists being assessed:** _____

_____

**Topic:** _____

| Criteria | Novice (Level I) | Apprentice (Level II) | Veteran (Level III) | Master (Level IV) |
|---|---|---|---|---|
| Picture Viewpoints | Two distinct viewpoints were not made or hardly noticeable as a comparison. (1–2 pts.) | Two distinct viewpoints were marginally made (3–4 pts.) | Two distinct viewpoints were clearly made (5–6 pts.) | Two distinct viewpoints were compared and contrasted with great detail. (7–8 pts.) |
| Paragraphs | Paragraphs were difficult to understand (1–3 pts.) | Paragraphs were marginally clear (4–6 pts.) | Paragraphs were understandable (7–9 pts.) | Paragraphs were clear and easy to understand (10–12 pts.) |
| **Comments and Total Points:** /20 pts. | | | | |

What I learned about the picture and its descriptive paragraph: _____

_____

_____

_____

What I learned about the second picture and its descriptive paragraph: _____

_____

_____

_____

# Examining Conflicts Arising from Diversity

## Objectives

- Students will identify a local or present day conflict arising from diverse viewpoints.
- Students will research the viewpoints represented to have a better understanding of the conflict.
- Students will participate in a magnetic debate in an effort to learn negotiating and listening skills.

## Standards

- McREL Civics, Level III, 11.3
- CCSS.ELA-Literacy.CCRA.R.1
- CCSS.ELA-Literacy.CCRA.SL.4

## Materials List

- Reproducibles (pages 128–130)
- Teacher Resources (page 131)
- index cards
- Internet access
- various print and online resources about the conflict

## Overarching Essential Question

What is civil war?

## Guiding Question

- Describe in detail some of the current civil wars worldwide.
- In what ways do diverse viewpoints play into waging war?
- For what reasons is the art of negotiation so vital in the prevention of a civil war?

## Suggested Schedule

The schedule below is based on a 45-minute period. If your school has block scheduling, please modify the schedule to meet your own needs.

| Day 1 | Day 2 | Day 3 | Day 4 | Day 5 |
|---|---|---|---|---|
| **Students brainstorm** possible **topics** about current-day **conflicts.** | **Students decide** on a **conflict topic** and **begin research** to find out the various viewpoints of the topic. | **Students conclude research** and then **write persuasive arguments** for an assigned side of the conflict. | **Students participate** in **a magnetic debate**. | **Students follow up with a discussion** about the conflict that was debated and then **reflect on the essential question**. |

# Examining Conflicts Arising from Diversity (cont.)

## Day 1

1. Remind students that a diversity of viewpoints was present in all of these lessons, and unfortunately, those diverse viewpoints led to the Civil War. In this simulation, students will learn the art of compromise and the ability to listen to multiple perspectives.

   - First, have students reflect on the different activities they examined while studying the Civil War. They began by looking at how diverse sides justified their viewpoints about slavery, as well as other issues leading up to the Civil War.

   - Then, students pretended to be Lincoln, who had to choose a general to lead Union troops. Have students recall the challenges of having to select someone who would be in charge of so many young lives.

   - Next, students assumed the role of soldiers on both the North and South sides during the Battle of Kaymat (Gettysburg).

   - Finally, utilizing Agam's fan fold design, students compared and contrasted various groups of people before and after the war.

2. Distribute copies of the *Brainstorming Conflicts* sheet (page 128). Challenge students to find a current conflict that the class can research. Tell students to use this page to brainstorm with others sitting nearby. Some students might want to look for conflicts online as they brainstorm.

3. Once students have had enough time to brainstorm topics, allow them to share these topics aloud while you chart it on the board. The class should vote to decide on a topic to research in the coming few days.

4. For homework, assign students the task of filling in the *Details About the Conflict* sheet (page 129). Both the teacher's and students' task will be to locate student-friendly background information on the conflict and to set up a workstation of resources.

## Day 2

1. Allow time for students to share what they found through their research and record it on a class chart.

2. Distribute copies of the *Magnetic Debate Notes* sheet (page 130). Decide on the two main positions of the conflict (*for and against*). The controversy should also be broken down into subcategories that can be argued for both the *for and against*. Work with the class to decide these categories and write them in the left column on the *Magnetic Debate Notes* sheet (page 130).

# Examining Conflicts Arising from Diversity (cont.)

3.  Divide the class into two groups. Half of the class will prepare for the *for* position, and the other half will prepare for the *against* position.

4.  Assign small groups for each category. Each category should have two contrasting positions. If you have a large class, you can assign more than one group to a category. Students with similar categories can compare notes.

5.  Give students time to perform their research (e.g., 30 minutes). This could also be a homework activity.

## Day 3

1.  Have students continue their research until they have enough information to write persuasive drafts for their topics. Before getting involved with the task, explain the simulation to them specifically. Then ask students to place themselves in the role of the teacher. During the simulation, what will you be assessing? What do they believe you will be looking for? Embark on the negotiable contracting of assessment. Use the criteria on the simulation day to assess how each student performs.

2.  Have students write their rough drafts for the one- or two-minute speeches and allow student peers to edit the speeches for clarity. Final drafts should be written and speeches should be memorized and practiced.

3.  Have students locate the key terms in their speeches and write these terms on index cards. These words will serve as prompts during the debate. Remind students to address the audience and keep their heads up so that they don't bore the class by speaking away from the audience in a head-hanging-down manner. Students should practice speaking using their index cards.

4.  Encourage students to add to their speeches by bringing in visuals such as graphs, video clips, pictures and other forms of items that will reinforce what they have to say. This can be completed for homework.

## Day 4

1.  On the day of the debate, distribute new copies of the *Magnetic Debate Notes* sheet (page 130) so that students can fill it out during the debate.

2.  Select an odd number of students (3, 5, or 7) representing both sides to serve as "undecideds." These students will not give their speeches, but rather serve as decision makers for the debate. Other members of their group will take over the speeches for the activity. The undecideds should clear their minds of all opinions on the topic.

# Examining Conflicts Arising from Diversity (cont.)

3. Select another small group that will serve as the "interrogation committee," asking questions for the students to debate.

4. To prepare the classroom, use masking tape to "draw" a line on the floor, dividing the class in half. Students who speak for the *for* side will sit on one side of the classroom and students who speak for the *against* side will sit on the other side of the classroom. The "undecideds" will place their chairs directly over the line of tape and sit down. See the *Classroom Layout* sheet (page 131) for an example of this layout.

5. Call out the first category and begin with the *for* point of view. The person who is responsible for this item will stand up and address the interrogation committee and the "undecideds." After the speech, the interrogation committee is allowed to ask one or two questions. Roam the room and assess the students while they perform.

6. A representative for this category from the *against* perspective will give a short rebuttal to what has been said. After the speech, the interrogation committee is allowed to ask one or two questions.

7. After the category has been completed, the undecideds should move their chairs about two feet closer to the group that has persuaded them. You may see the chair move in one direction for part of the class and then back in the other direction during the later part of the presentations. As the sides debate, all students should complete the *Magnetic Debate Notes* sheet (page 130).

8. Call the next category, but let the *against* point of view begin, followed by the *for* point of view. Alternate for each turn.

9. After all categories have been heard, the side to which the largest number of undecideds have moved their chairs toward wins the debate.

## Day 5

1. Have students reflect on the debate from the previous day and on the arguments they witnessed through a class discussion. Chart their negotiable points on the board.

2. Remind students that part of being a citizen in the world entails striving to understand diverse viewpoints within conflicts, just as they examined the diverse viewpoints in the Civil War conflict.

3. End with a final discussion or ticket-out-the-door using the overarching essential question *Compare and contrast what you knew about the Civil War before we started the unit to what you know about it today.*

# Brainstorming Conflicts

**Directions:** Use this page to brainstorm possible topics about current day conflicts.

| Possible Topics of Conflicts | What I Know About This Topic |
|---|---|
| | |
| | |
| | |
| | |
| | |
| | |
| | |

# Details About the Conflict

**Directions:** Find at least five details about this conflict.  Elaborate on these details in the space provided.

**Conflict:** _____

| Details About the Conflict | What I Know and Understand About This Conflict |
|---|---|
| 1. | |
| 2. | |
| 3. | |
| 4. | |
| 5. | |

# Magnetic Debate Notes

**Directions:** Use this page to organize your thoughts during the Magnetic Debate.

| Category | Pro | Con |
|---|---|---|
|  |  |  |
|  |  |  |
|  |  |  |
|  |  |  |
|  |  |  |
|  |  |  |
|  |  |  |
|  |  |  |

# Classroom Layout

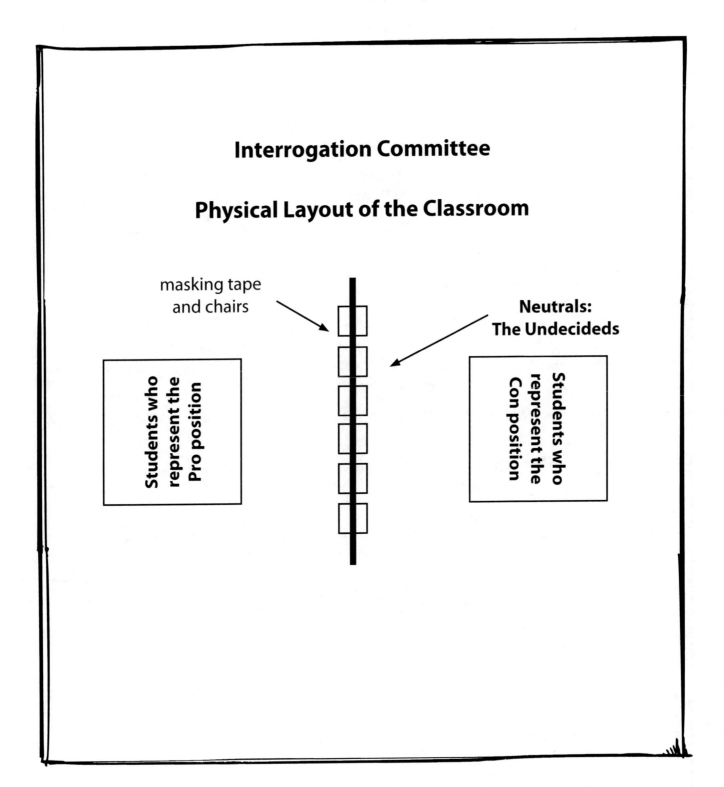

**Interrogation Committee**

**Physical Layout of the Classroom**

masking tape
and chairs

Neutrals:
The Undecideds

Students who
represent the
Pro position

Students who
represent the
Con position

# References Cited

Conklin, Wendy, and Andi Stix. 2014. *Active Learning Across the Content Areas*. Huntington Beach, CA: Shell Education.

Crane, Thomas. 2002. *The Heart of Coaching: Using Transformation Coaching to Create a High-Performance Culture*. San Diego, CA: FTA Press.

Danielson, Charlotte. 2011. "The Framework for Teaching." The Danielson Group. http://www.danielsongroup.org/article.aspx?page=frameworkforteaching.

Jacobs, Heidi H. 2010. *Curriculum 21: Essential Education for a Changing World*. Alexandria, VA: Association for Supervision and Curriculum Development.

King, F. J., Ludwika Goodson, and Faranak Rohani. 1998. *Higher-Order Thinking Skills*. Tallahassee, FL: Center for Advancement of Learning and Assessment.

Kise, Jane A. G. 2006. *Differentiated Coaching: A Framework for Helping Teachers Change*. Thousand Oaks, CA: Corwin Press.

Latrhop, L., Vincent, C., and Annette M. Zehler. 1993. *Special Issues Analysis Center Focus Group Report: Active Learning Instructional Models for Limited English Proficient (LEP) Students*. Report to U.S. Department of Education, Office of Bilingual Education and Minority Languages Affairs (OBEMLA). Arlington, VA: Development Associates, Inc.

Michalko, Michael. 2006. *Thinkertoys: A Handbook of Creative-Thinking Techniques*. Berkeley, CA: Ten Speed Press.

National Council for the Social Studies. 2008. "A Vision of Powerful Teaching and Learning in the Social Studies: Building Social Understanding and Civic Efficacy." Position statement. http://www.ncss.org/positions/powerful.

Scriven, Michael, and Richard Paul. 1987. "Defining Critical Thinking." Dillion Beach, CA: National Council for Excellence in Critical Thinking Instruction. 1996. http://www.criticalthinking.org.

Stix, Andi. 2012. "Essential and Guiding Questions." *Stix Pix for the Interactive Classroom*. Accessed April 29. http://www.andistix.com/essential_and_guiding_questions.

Stix, Andi, and Frank Hrbek.1999. "A Rubric Bank for Teachers." *The Interactive Classroom*. Accessed on August 14. http://www.andistix.com.

———. 2006. *Teachers as Classroom Coaches*. Alexandria VA: Association for Supervision and Curriculum Development.

Zmuda, Allison. 2008. "Springing into Active Learning." *Educational Leadership* 66 (3): 38–42.

# About the Authors

**Andi Stix Ed.D., and PCC,** is a national educational consultant, administrator, teacher, and certified life and instructional coach. In addition to teaching for over 35 years, Dr. Stix has been a presenter at seminars and a keynote speaker. Andi earned her doctorate in Gifted Education from Columbia University and currently owns and operates the Interactive Classroom, an education-consulting firm in New Rochelle, New York. Dr. Stix founded and runs the award-winning afterschool enrichment program for bright, curious, and clever-minded children, G·tec Kids. Through her work, Andi continues to be an advocate for Synergy Westchester where she focuses on the needs of teachers and families of gifted learners. Her articles have appeared in *Social Education*, *Middle School Journal*, *Social Studies*, *Arithmetic Teacher*, *The Math Notebook*, *ERIC*, and *Gems of AGATE*. Along with her co-author, Frank Hrbek, Andi has written *Teachers as Classroom Coaches*, which focuses on integrating coaching strategies into the fabric of the educational system. Together, they have also written the *Exploring History* series of simulations and hands-on investigations in history for the secondary school market. For her work in professional development, Andi received the Alexinia Baldwin Educator of the Year Award. Books Dr. Stix has authored include *Using Literature and Simulations in Your Social Studies Classroom*, *Integrated Cooperative Strategies for the Social Studies, Language Arts, and the Humanities*. For fun and useful activities, please refer to Andi Stix's blog at andistix.com.

**Frank Hrbek, M.A.,** is the co-author of the *Exploring History* and *Active History* series. A well-established educator, Mr. Hrbek has spent the past 40 years teaching middle school social studies in New York City. He holds a Master of Arts in History after having received a degree in English, with minors in journalism and history, at New York University. Mr. Hrbek works alongside Dr. Stix, attending workshops, conferences, and presenting at colleges. He has successfully integrated many of Dr. Stix's new coaching and cooperative learning strategies in his own classroom. Their series, *Exploring History*, is a three-time winner of the New York State's Social Studies Program of Excellence Award, as well as Middle States Council for the Social Studies' Social Studies Program of Excellence Certificate. The series also received the Outstanding Curriculum Development Award from the National Association of Gifted Children, and is a two-time winner of the Teacher's Choice Award from Learning magazine.

# Contents of the Digital Resource CD

| | Reproducibles and Resources | |
|---|---|---|
| Page | Activity Sheet | Filename/Folder Name |
| 25–28 | Civil War Background Information | civilwarinfo.pdf |
| 29 | How Slavery Was Affected | slavery.pdf |
| 30 | Dred Scott Case Background Information | dredscottinfo.pdf |
| 31–32 | Dred Scott, A Slave | dredscottslave.pdf |
| 33–34 | Ellis Wilson, A Northerner | ewilson.pdf |
| 35–36 | Marcus Thompson, A Southerner | mthompson.pdf |
| 37–38 | J.F.A. Sanford, Abolitionist and New Owner of Dred Scott | sanford.pdf |
| 39–40 | A Slave Auctioneer's Letter to the Birmingham Sentinel | auctioneer.pdf |
| 41–42 | Perspective Discussion Questions | perspective.pdf |
| 43 | The Ruling on Dred Scott | dredscottruling.pdf |
| 44 | Dred Scott Discussion Assessment | dredscottassess.pdf |
| 49 | Carousel Brainstorm Activity Questions | carousel.pdf |
| 50–55 | Candidate Profile Cards | candidateprof.pdf |
| 56 | Candidate Comparison Chart | candidatecomp.pdf |
| 57 | Vote for a General Questions | votequestions.pdf |
| 58 | Vote for a General Results Chart | voteresults.pdf |
| 65 | What Really Happened? | what.pdf |
| 70–71 | Battle Vocabulary Cards | battlevocab.pdf |
| 72–73 | Battle of Kaymat Background Information | battleinfo.pdf |
| 74 | Battle of Kaymat Map | battlemap.pdf |
| 75 | Battle of Kaymat Map with Markers | battlemarkers.pdf |
| 76 | Battle of Kaymat Map Key | battlekey.pdf |
| 77 | Battle of Kaymat Spinner | battlespinner.pdf |
| 78 | How to Play the Game | howtoplay.pdf |
| 79–99 | Battle of Kaymat Dispatches and Spin Cards | battledispatch.pdf |

# Contents of the Digital Resource CD *(cont.)*

| Reproducibles and Resources | | |
|---|---|---|
| **Page** | **Activity Sheet** | **Filename/Folder Name** |
| 100 | Soldier Fate Sheet | soldier.pdf |
| 101–105 | Generals' Decisions of Action | generals.pdf |
| 106–109 | Whole-Class Discussion Questions | wholeclass.pdf |
| 114 | People Affected by the Civil War | people.pdf |
| 115 | Civil War Venn Diagram | civilwarvenn.pdf |
| 118–121 | Fan Fold Design Instructions<br>Fan Fold Lined Paper | fanfoldinstruct.pdf<br>linedpaper.doc |
| 122 | Displaying Your Fan Fold Design | fanfolddisplay.pdf |
| 123 | Peer Assessment of Fan Fold Designs | fanfoldassess.pdf<br>fanfoldassess.doc |
| 128 | Brainstorming Conflicts | brainstorm.pdf |
| 129 | Details About the Conflict | conflictdetails.pdf |
| 130 | Magnetic Debate Notes | magnetic.pdf |
| 131 | Classroom Layout | classlayout.pdf |

| Teacher Resources | |
|---|---|
| **Activity Sheet** | **Filename/Folder Name** |
| Rubric Bank for Teachers | rubricbank.pdf<br>rubricbank.doc |
| GOPER Model | gopermodel.pdf |

| Correlation Charts | |
|---|---|
| **Correlation Charts** | **Filename/Folder Name** |
| CCSS, WIDA, TESOL, McREL, and NCSS | standards.pdf |

# Notes